THE DRACULA SCRAPBOOK

THE
DRACULA
SCRAPBOOK

PETER HAINING

LONGMEADOW
PRESS

This 1992 edition published by
Longmeadow Press
201 High Ridge Road
Stamford, CT 06904

by arrangement with Octopus Illustrated Publishing
part of Reed International Books

ISBN 0-681-41643-2

Printed in China

0987654321

For Gerry Battye
who can get blood out
of any audience!

'Dracula offers the illusion of immortality, the subconscious wish we all have for limitless life. He is a man of tremendous brain and physical strength, with a strange dark heroism. He is either a reincarnation or he has never died. He is a superman image with erotic appeal for women who find him totally alluring. In many ways he is everything people would like to be—the anti-hero or heroic villain—and, like the much maligned Rasputin, he is part saint, part sinner. Men also find him irresistible because they cannot stop him.'

Christopher Lee

Acknowledgements

The author would like to extend his thanks to the following individuals and organisations for their help in the writing of this book. In particular Christopher Lee, Peter Cushing, John Carradine, Lord Olivier, William Marshall, Frank Langella, Carol Borland, Barbara Shelley, Barbara Steele, Enno Patalas, Werner Herzog and Klaus Kinski. Also for their help in my research, W.O.G. Lofts; Bruce Wightman and Robert James Leake of the Dracula Society; Bruce Francis and John McLaughlin of The Book Sail; Kurt Singer of BP Singer Features Inc.; Tony Whitehead, Brian Inglis, Daniel Farson, James Drummond, Ivan Stokes Dixon, Tim Ostinrein, Al Smith, Dr David H. Dolphin and Ed Kosterville. Several other correspondents in America and Europe who also greatly assisted me have asked to remain anonymous, but they still have my sincere thanks.

I am also grateful to the following publications for allowing me to quote from their pages: *The Observer, The Guardian, The Times, Punch, The Sunday Times, London Evening Standard, New Society* and *Film Weekly*. And to these film companies for allowing the use of stills from their films: Universal Pictures, Hammer Films, Prana Films, MGM, Columbia Pictures, Embassy Films, American-International Pictures, Curtis Productions, 20th Century Fox and Graphis Films.

Last, but not least, I must record my particular appreciation to the staffs of the following libraries who were generous with their time and knowledge while I was consulting their invaluable archives of books and manuscripts: The British Library, London; Whitby Public Library, Yorkshire; Rosenbach Library, Philadelphia; and the Library of Congress in Washington, DC.

6

Contents

Dracula Lives!

Over one hundred years ago, in the autumn of 1887, the vampire Count Dracula left the fastness of his Transylvanian castle and stalked the streets of London—thereby starting a legend which has turned him into one of the most famous fictional characters in the world. Introduced in the pages of a Victorian novel, he has since been transposed into all the media of entertainment and earned such acclaim that the *Sunday Times* could comment in August 1985:

> The Dracula myth, along with Tarzan, Sherlock Holmes and Superman, continues to hold public imagination. The evil Count has appeared in over 200 films from at least 10 countries, in plays, comics and on television. The Bram Stoker novel has never been out of print. Commercial packaging now even includes package holidays to Dracula's Rumanian castle.

To this statement one might add that the original novel has been translated into 22 languages, selling in 91 separate editions throughout 47 countries. Variations on the theme have also appeared in more than 30 novels, at least 120 short stories, uncounted newspaper and magazine articles, plus five television series reaching 430 million viewers of 17 nations! No small achievement for a tale the author thought *might* prove a better-than-average potboiler on a subject that was not exactly new . . .

The legend of vampires has existed for centuries all over the world, but in Britain, in that year of 1887, it took on a wholly new aspect. For what Stoker did was to turn an undead creature of the night, which tradition said was a marauding fiend ever on the search for human blood, into a refined and aristocratic nobleman. A fatal man, to be sure, a charming, intelligent host who totally unnerved his victims with his unique blend of sado-eroticism. And although, at the close of the novel, he was apparently dispatched by his nemesis, Professor Van Helsing, he has never ceased to stalk the imagination of each passing generation.

The achievement of this single work is all the more remarkable when you consider the enormous changes which have taken place in our attitudes: a point well made by R. W. Johnson in an article entitled 'The Myth of the 20th Century', in *New Society*, December 9, 1982:

> In a cultural sense, the 20th century has been the great age of debunking,

Bram Stoker, the man
who created Dracula,
and a centenary
signature from the
Lyceum Theatre
where he worked the
year the vampire
Count stalked London.

of secularisation and de-mythologisation. It is not just that we believe less
in gods and superstitions: it is impossible now for racial mythologies
about Jews, Aryans and blacks to get a respectable hearing; and in large
areas of social and private life the old taboos have fallen like sandcastles
before the advancing tide of rationalism. In a sense, we are all agnostics
now.

There is one great exception to this: the vampire myth. To be sure, the
myth is hardly a modern creation. But the audience and resonance this
myth has achieved in the 20th century is quite unparalleled.

Johnson rightly points out that there had been vampire novels before—
ranging from that brief and light-weight tale *The Vampyre* (1819) by John
William Polidori, the friend of Shelley and Lord Byron, which was created at
that famous soirée in Switzerland which also produced Frankenstein, brain-
child of Shelley's teenage wife; to the almost interminably long 'penny dreadful', *Varney the Vampire, or The Feast of Blood* by Thomas Prest (1847); but it was
Bram Stoker who happened along at the crucial moment.

In a way (Johnson continues), Bram Stoker was simply lucky. The first
stage of de-mystification is to bring a subject out into the full serious light.
Stoker wrote a 'serious' tragedy about vampires, and the 20th century,

9

A vampire play—incorrectly ascribed to Lord Byron—which Bram Stoker almost certainly knew about and may well have utilised.

which de-mythologises everything, was ready to begin the long process of accepting—and thus defusing—the most powerful subterranean myth of all. By the 1970s and 1980s we have actually got round to really funny films about vampires—not burlesques, which refuse to take the myth seriously, but comedies which accept the myth head on, and still laugh at it. Seen in this light, Stoker was simply the man who brought the myth to the surface of the real literary world and caught the wave.

Of course, he also struck a basic human chord: our attraction to fictional horror, whether or not we have actually experienced the real thing.

Tony Whitehead, a consultant psychiatrist who has made a special study of what he calls 'our love affair with Dracula', explains it like this:

The attraction is complex and varies from one individual to another. However, there are certain consistent elements: the stimulation of a sensation of fear, the stirring up of primitive superstitions which lie dormant within all of us, the simplification of concepts of good and evil, suppressed facets of the sexual drive, and the enjoyment of other people's misery. Some people risk their lives to feel fear, but most welcome the sensation if it can be engendered without hazard.

As prime examples of this, Whitehead cites scenes in which Dracula approaches a beautiful young victim, intent on sinking his teeth into her neck, only to be repelled by the crucifix she is wearing:

Here we have suspense and a build-up of terror which creates within us the bodily changes associated with fear. This includes an increased heart rate, a surge of blood to our muscles—and a tingling sensation of the skin caused by muscles at the base of our hair trying to make our hair stand on end. That prickling feeling has its origins in our animal ancestors. Animals respond to fear by raising their fur, so increasing their protection if attacked. The primitive mechanism is active in man in spite of being unable to protect himself. Perspiring when we are afraid is possibly more useful to us because it makes the skin slippery and less easy to grasp.

He has also commented on Dracula's ability to change into and out of the form of a bat as another important element. 'Scenes like this contain the important element of magic,' he says. 'The ability to change from man to beast is a well-established part of our mythology and our primitive memory recalls our fears of witchcraft.'

Of the scenes in which the vampire attacks and actually sinks his fangs into the neck of his victim, he says:

Blood has great symbolic significance, of course. It is let in primitive sacrifice and associated with the defloration of virgins. Attila drank it to

Dracula one hundred years on and as topical as ever—a cartoon from the London *Evening Standard* of January 7, 1987, during the campaign against AIDS.

11

give him superhuman strength. The sight of it makes some of us faint. There is also overt sexuality in this scene and often pleasure is portrayed in the vampire and the victim, so illustrating both sadism and masochism.

If he were alive today, Bram Stoker would no doubt be amazed and even a little amused at the stir his book has caused. In fact, he died on April 20, 1912 when the century he has so influenced was scarcely under way. The original novel was first published, in June 1897, at a price of six shillings—thirty pence by today's coinage! Stoker wrote his book as just one more novel among those he turned out over the years—as a form of relaxation and to supplement his living as a theatrical manager—but more than any of the others it was deeply rooted both in real people and places, and in actual events. It was a fusion of his own imagination and well-researched facts. It was also, consciously or unconsciously, tapped from the deep well-springs of his own strange personality.

The life of Abraham Stoker, who was born on November 8, 1847, at 15, The Crescent, Clontarf in Dublin, has been more than fully covered in two biographies—not to mention innumerable essays and articles—and here I intend to do no more than sketch in the bare facts.

Stoker's father, also Abraham, was one of the officials in the Chief Secretary's Department in Dublin Castle, and the boy was initially launched on a similar career after completing his education at Trinity College. In childhood he was sickly for a number of years, but he overcame this handicap by determinedly throwing himself into various sports and in time developed a strong body and vibrant personality. He left Trinity College with honours in science, mathematics, oratory, history and composition and, as stipulated by his parents, went to work in the Irish Civil Service.

The work did not satisfy him for long, however, and to while away the boredom of the job he began writing short essays and stories for the Dublin newspapers, and for magazines such as *The Shamrock* and *The Warder*. In September 1872 he published his first tale, 'The Crystal Cup', a grim fantasy which indicated the direction of his fictional interests. Other similar stories followed, like 'Buried Treasures' (*The Shamrock*, March 1875), 'The Chain of Destiny' (*The Shamrock*, May 1875) and 'The Dualitists; or, The Death Doom of the Double Born', a real shocker for *The Theatre Annual* of 1887, containing several elements of bloodshed and cruelty which were to be given fuller expression in the later story of Dracula.

During this period Stoker also began developing a passion for the theatre and contributed reviews on various local productions to the *Dublin Mail*. These reports showed a genuine understanding of drama, and were directly responsible for bringing him into contact with the great English actor, Sir Henry Irving, when he came with his company to perform in Ireland in 1876. Within a short time the two men had become friends, and Stoker decided to 'throw in his lot' with the actor (to quote one account); he was to be Sir Henry's manager and

The haunt of Dracula. Inside the vampire's castle in Transylvania in the original 1931 film with Bela Lugosi and Helen Chandler.

confidential secretary for the rest of the latter's life.

In Bram Stoker's obituary, published in *The Times* on April 22, 1912, there is a colourful account of this association:

Few men have played the part of *fidus Achates* to a great personality with more gusto. Mr. Stoker must have found his new life thoroughly congenial. He shared Irving's counsels in all his enterprises; went about with him in the closest relationships of confidential friend and right-hand man; assisted at the many brilliant entertainments which his chief gave during the heyday of The Lyceum in London; met and was cordially treated by people of all sorts and conditions; and knew thoroughly the ins and outs of the financial side of the riskiest of all professions. From 1878, the year in which Irving became lessee and manager of The Lyceum, to 1905, when he died, the takings exceeded two millions. When the crash came, Stoker remained loyally at his friend's side, during years which would have been fatal to less enduring spirits by the contrast which they afforded to the dazzling triumphs which preceded them.

In the midst of all this hectic activity, Stoker managed to find time to marry a beautiful young girl named Florence Anne Lemon, a Colonel's daughter, and not long afterwards the couple had a son, Noel Thornley. He also expanded his literary output by producing a number of fantasy novels which began with *Under The Sunset* in 1882, continued with *The Snake's Pass* in 1891, *The Shoulder of Shasta* in 1895, and then reached their apogee with *Dracula* which appeared in 1897.

The book which was to change our perception of vampires was greeted guardedly by the critics. The powerful *Athenaeum*'s reviewer, for instance, wrote: 'Mr. Stoker is the purveyor of so many strange wares that Dracula reads like a determined effort to go, as it were, "one better" than others in the same field. How far the author is himself a believer in the phenomena described is not for the reviewer to say.' *Punch* was similarly reserved: 'It is a pity that Mr. Bram Stoker was not content to employ such supernatural anti-vampire receipts as his wildest imagination might have invented without rashly venturing on a domain where angels fear to tread.'

Stoker's employer, Sir Henry Irving, was shamelessly damning, flinging down his copy of the book with the one word, 'Dreadful!' He was no more impressed when Stoker staged a four-hour reading of the novel at The Lyceum to establish his theatrical copyright.

Little did Irving—or Stoker, for that matter—imagine that in the fullness of time the book was to become a staple drama for the stage, and beyond that on

The Count's lair in the latest version of the novel filmed by John Badham in 1979.

films and television. Only the author's mother seems to have appreciated just how important a book her son had written, and although her judgement might well have been biased by maternal pride, it certainly foresaw what the future held.

'No book since Mrs. Shelley's *Frankenstein* or indeed any other at all has come near yours in originality or terror,' she wrote in haste from her home in Dublin, and added as if to underline her words, 'Poe is nowhere!'

During those closing years of the Victorian era, however, it was the fate of *Dracula* to be marked down as little more than a 'highly sensational novel'— although it did continue to sell well and was certainly the most successful of Stoker's twenty books. Not until the new century was it to find its true place in literary history.

There is no one alive today to recall Bram Stoker and the effect this reception had on him, although writer Brian Inglis has an interesting comment to make on the man and his times:

> He was a friend of my grand-parents, and as I recollect his brother was their doctor. They spoke of him with the kind of rueful condescension reserved for Irish scapegraces who were obviously destined for a sticky end, because they got mixed up with the Stage and other forms of vice. So he surprised everyone by writing a best seller.

Another author and broadcaster, Daniel Farson, who is Stoker's great-nephew, sees him as a much more complex man than that:

> He was two people. Outwardly bluff and hearty. Inwardly, he needed release. Throughout his life he was deeply conscious of personal honour, of being a gentleman, of the sacred nature of the female sex. This was a resolute façade—but it concealed a man who was highly disturbed. All of his books reflect this Jekyll and Hyde nature—but none more so than *Dracula*. For sheer horror and sex it can't be improved.

Farson has carried out extensive research into the life of his famous relative and has come to the conclusion that, to a considerable degree, *Dracula* was created out of this frustration:

> From my research, and from what my grandmother, Enid Stoker, told me, I had the strong impression that my great-aunt, Florence, Bram Stoker's wife, was a very cold woman indeed. This has been confirmed by a recent conversation with their granddaughter, who told me that she doubted if 'Granny Moo', as she called Florence, was really capable of love. She was cursed with great beauty and needed to maintain it. Consequently she was vain. 'In my knowledge now,' said her granddaughter, 'she was very anti-sex after having my father when she was twenty. I think she was quite put off.' She thought it probable that Florence refused to have sex again with Bram after their son was born.

> This revelation exceeded my suspicions. It confirms Bram's sexual frustration and explains the obsession with the 'ideal' woman, so unnatur-

ally feminine, in his books. Poor Bram married to frigid Florence; Beauty and the Beast [. . .] Bram Stoker's personal frustration is easily understandable in the context of those schizophrenic Victorian times. It is our good fortune that he realised it in the masterpiece of *Dracula*.

While agreeing with this theory, I believe that *Dracula* was also a concoction of people and legends from Rumania mixed with a knowledge of locations—London in particular—to give the whole story the air of verisimilitude. Stoker reasoned, quite correctly, that if he was writing a 'serious' novel he had to convince the reader that the core of the book was authentic and that his characters were believable people.

Curiously, despite the fact that Stoker never visited Rumania to gather information for his book, the novel has had a profound effect upon that country. For he incorporated a legendary Rumanian 'hero', Vlad Dracula, or Vlad the Impaler, in his creation of Dracula, and each year tourists in ever-increasing numbers flock to the country to see the carefully catalogued haunts of the vampire count. Although not exactly turning people away, the Rumanians are said to be growing a little weary of the Dracula cult.

One observer, Adrian Paunescu, writing in the magazine *Contemporanul* in August 1986, described *Dracula* as 'political pornography directed against us by our neighbours'. It was, he said, part of a concerted campaign 'by reactionaries of every colour to slander the very idea of being a Rumanian as well as the eternal idea of Rumania.'

No mention was made of just how many years the book which was accused of causing such an upheaval had been around. This was picked up by Dan Ionescu of Radio Free Europe who countered pointedly by remarking on the facilities being given to 'Dracula Tours', which brought the country much-needed foreign currency.

'The only thing that has gone,' he said, 'are the days when an off-duty cook

Members of the Dracula Society on tour in the Carpathian Mountains, Transylvania, in October 1974, near the location of Count Dracula's castle. The cloaked guide, Peter Sipeiu, is holding a 'Pobber's Steak' of charcoal-grilled mixed meats!

from a hotel in the Carpathians used to pop up out of a coffin to thrill the odd foreign visitors. Nowadays it is a skilfully organised operation under the aegis of the Tourist Office.'

The world-wide success of Dracula has led, inevitably, to other claims being made to his ancestry—primarily that he is of Scottish or Irish descent.

James Drummond, a Scottish writer and researcher, believes Stoker drew his inspiration from holidays spent north of the border:

> The real Dracula country is in Scotland: more precisely the north-east corner of Buchan. It was here, on the rocky headland to the north of Cruden Bay, that Bram Stoker found during the first of several holidays in 1893, the castle that was to haunt his dreams, and the dreams of generations of readers. Slains Castle, gaunt and windswept, hanging on the edge of jagged cliffs, with gulls sweeping and screaming round its bleak, cold battlements, and the sea breaking on the rocks below . . .
>
> The legend of Slains (is) about a haunting, not by a ghost, but by the 'undead' body of a man whose soul had gone before him to the other world. In using the legend as the basis for *Dracula*, Stoker transported the main action to Transylvania and then to Whitby, although he had at first planned to leave the story in its Scottish setting.
>
> Perhaps it was his showman's instinctive feeling for a colourful setting that prompted him to choose Rumania. Or it may have been that, loving Cruden Bay so much, he could not bring himself to make it, even in fiction, the crucible of evil.

Convinced though Drummond may be, I believe it was not *Dracula* but Stoker's later novel, *The Mystery of the Sea* (1902)—which *is* actually set in Cruden Bay—that was sparked off by these holidays.

Nor, I am afraid, am I any more convinced by the claim of Ivan Stokes Dixon, another great-nephew of Stoker, that Dracula is actually Irish:

> Dracula was born in the mind of an Irishman—therefore he is Irish. The Rumanians get a lot of money out of tourists, but the truth is that Bram Stoker never visited their country. He got his information from guide books. I want the Irish Tourist Board to set up a Bram Stoker Museum so that we can have some of the credit for this remarkable work.

One of Dixon's claims is certainly true—that Bram Stoker got his information about Rumania from tourist guide books. He used other sources, too, both in London and Whitby where parts of the story of Dracula are indisputably laid.

Now, following the extraordinary discovery of the original manuscript of the book—which has been lying forgotten in a trunk for perhaps half a century or more—it is at last possible to pin-point the original sources, people and places which inspired this dark masterpiece, and also to relate the curious events which took place in 1887 and caused Bram Stoker to set his tale in that particular year . . .

2

An Amazing Story of Resurrection

It was a bright spring morning on one of the typical picturesque farms which dot the rural north-western region of Pennsylvania. From the outside, the farm, with its huddle of Dutch barns and fields given over mainly to dairying and a little agriculture, was like many others in this part of the United States.

But on this particular day one of the most extraordinary and unsuspected discoveries in the history of literature was about to be made.

In accordance with the wishes of those concerned, it is not possible for me to reveal either the precise location of this farm or the name of the family who were living there, but I *can* assure the reader of the absolute authenticity of what follows.

The farm had been in the possession of the same family for several generations and, as often happens in such cases, one of the barns had been given over to storing a whole variety of old items and belongings discarded over the years. On the day in question, two members of the family had decided to satisfy their idle curiosity and look through the contents of the barn. It was not that they expected to find anything valuable, but there were some old trunks piled up at the back, which they had noticed from time to time and which seemed worth investigating.

On clearing aside the general clutter, three trunks were found and hauled out into the daylight. Then, brushing off the dust and easing up the old clasps, the two explorers opened each one in turn.

The first looked unexciting enough: a bundle of small, innocuous personal items and a large sheaf of papers. The second was more promising: packed to the lid with an assortment of clothes, some obviously of considerable age although still in good condition.

But it was when the third trunk was opened that the couple stood back with a mixture of surprise and revulsion on their faces. For inside lay a quantity of *dead rats*!

'I know it sounds wild,' an informant who investigated this find told me, 'but I am not making this story up. The rat corpses had evidently been there for quite some time—based on the fact that they were quite dry and withered from the description I was given.'

My informant has no doubt that they *were* rats—and not any other kind of small creatures—and that they had evidently been deliberately placed in the trunk rather than having found their own way in. But *why* should anyone want to keep a trunkful of rats?

That, however, was not to be the biggest surprise; indeed the next discovery served to make the trunk of rats seem still more bizarre.

When the couple had got over their amazement and carefully shut the trunk, they turned their attention to the clothes and, finally, to the items in the first trunk.

On closer examination, the sheaf of papers proved more interesting than they had thought, for it was obviously a manuscript, quite old, and typewritten. A quick flip through the yellowing leaves revealed a multitude of pen and blue pencil marks and corrections, and the pages had evidently been cut and re-pasted together numerous times. There was a smudged and grubby title page, too, on which had been written in a far from clear hand:

THE UN-DEAD.

Looking closer, the couple thought at first glance that the line below this title read 'By Barn Stoker', but an 'r' had apparently been smudged by the writer's pen, and the name was more likely 'Bram Stoker'. Below this were the words, 'Author of *Under the Sunset*, *The Snake's Pass*, *The Watter's Mou* and *The Shoulder of Shasta*'. A final line added, 'Copyright 1897 By Bram Stoker. All Rights Reserved.'

Neither of the two people was a great reader, but the name Bram Stoker rang a bell. Hadn't he written a book called *Dracula*, about vampires, one of them suggested? Perhaps, then, this was the manuscript of *another* of his titles?

What those Pennsylvanians did not know then—but soon afterwards discovered—was that they had stumbled upon the original manuscript of one of the great classics of horror literature. For, as had been well known for many years, when Bram Stoker signed a contract for his soon-to-be-famous book on May 20, 1897, with the London publishers, Archibald Constable & Company of 2, Whitehall Gardens, Westminster, the provisional title was given as 'The Un-Dead'. It was only shortly before publication, when the book was already in galley, that the change to *Dracula* was made—at whose insistence, publisher or author, we shall probably never know.

It was clearly a find of the first magnitude, for it was generally believed that the original manuscript had long since been lost. An entry in the *Modern Library in First Editions* catalogue (1938) is typical: 'So far as we can discover, the final manuscript for Dracula is no longer in existence.' Indeed, it seemed that only Stoker's original notes for the novel had survived, and these had been sold at Sotheby's on July 7, 1913—the year after the author's death—for the princely sum of two guineas: two pounds and ten pence in today's coinage. Sixty years later these papers came into the possession of the Rosenbach Library, also in Pennsylvania, in Philadelphia, where they still remain. (These papers will be more fully dealt with in the next chapter.)

The manuscript of *The Un-Dead* was, naturally, subjected to the most intense scrutiny by both handwriting and literary experts to establish its provenance,

Front cover of the very rare special edition of *Dracula's Guest*, issued to mark the 250th performance of the stage play of Dracula.

Dracula's Guest

by

Bram Stoker

250TH LONDON PERFORMANCE
OF "Dracula"

PRINCE OF WALES' THEATRE
SOUVENIR EDITION
1927

but the deeper the investigation went the more the mystery grew and the more questions seemed to be unanswerable . . .

The manuscript consists of a total of 529 pages which vary in size from eight and a half inches by ten inches to as much as 14 and a half inches. It is typed, although extensively annotated with handwritten corrections and revisions.

A point of particular interest is that it must qualify as one of the earliest novels to have been type-written. Victorian novelists at the close of the last century were still almost all writing their books in longhand, so Stoker can be seen as something of a pioneer in this respect. Perhaps because he travelled so much, it was necessary for him to work this way. That Stoker was interested in this new labour-saving device—the first shift-key models had appeared in 1878—is clear from the fact that one is mentioned in *Dracula* itself: the 'Traveller's Typewriter' which Mina Harker uses.

The condition of the manuscript, and the number of pages that have obviously been re-numbered and re-assembled with scissors and paste, suggest that Stoker carried out extensive revision of his narrative. Or was it *someone else* who did this?

I only pose this question because a story has long persisted in fantasy fiction circles that the first draft of Stoker's novel was completely unpublishable and had to be thoroughly worked upon by another hand. The famous horror story writer, H. P. Lovecraft (1890–1937), who actually lived not far from Pennsylvania, at Providence on Rhode Island, was at the bottom of this story, having once claimed that he had 'an acquaintance who was contacted about the job of revising *Dracula*.'

The discovery of this manuscript and the condition it is in rather seems to scotch this particular rumour, particularly as the annotations have been identified as the handwriting of Stoker himself. The only others in blue pencil are clearly those of the editor at Archibald Constable, who prepared the work for press.

Another fascinating point to emerge is that Stoker evidently wrote large chunks of the book at great speed, leaving gaps where he required additional facts to authenticate the story, which could be added later after he had researched them. He appears to have carried out all the necessary research himself—although he did consult one expert. Clearly marked on the pages dealing with blood transfusions and autopsies are the notes and suggestions of a surgeon who must have read the manuscript. These annotations have then been incorporated by Stoker into the text.

Although it is clear that Stoker had most of his characters and settings well defined before he began writing—there are, for example, so few changes to either Count Dracula or Dr Van Helsing that they obviously stepped fully formed from his imagination—a few significant changes were made, primarily in certain locations and even in one major character. Renfield, the Count's unbalanced 'disciple', is referred to variously in this first version as 'The Flyman', Renfold or sometimes just by a blank space. It must have been a

The Count Dracula-
like character, Edgar
Caswall, who
appeared in Bram
Stoker's later vampire
novel, *The Lair of the
White Worm* (1911).

23

happy moment for Stoker when the name Renfield finally crystallised in his mind!

There is undeniable evidence, too, that Stoker made a number of cuts in the story—dropping words here, lines there, and even a few complete episodes. The most important of these cuts occurs at the very beginning of the book and amounts to a considerable number of pages. This provides confirmation of another long-held belief, that Stoker was asked to cut an entire section of his book by his publishers to conform to the 390-page extent they had in mind as being economically viable for their proposed print run of 3,000 copies. What he deleted was the section later published as a short story, 'Dracula's Guest', in a posthumous anthology of his work assembled under that title by his wife.

Another excision is rather more inexplicable, for it is a spectacular description of the destruction of Dracula's Castle; I am at a loss to understand *why* Stoker decided on omitting this vivid piece of prose. Only the first sentence of the extract below has survived on the penultimate page of 'Mina Harker's Journal' in the published book.

> The castle of Dracula now stood out against the red sun and every stone of its broken battlements was articulated against the light. As we looked there came a terrible convulsion of the earth so that we seemed to rock to and fro and fell to our knees. At the same moment, with a roar that seemed to shake the very heavens, the whole castle and the rock and even the hill on which it stood, seemed to rise into the air and scatter in fragments, while a mighty cloud of black and yellow smoke, volume on volume, in rolling grandeur, was shot upwards with inconceivable rapidity. Then there was a stillness in nature as the echoes of that thunderous report seemed to come as with the hollow boom of a thunder-clap—the long reverberating roll which seems as though the floors of heaven shook. Then, down in a mighty ruin falling whence they rose, came the fragments that had been tossed skyward in the cataclysm.
>
> From where we stood it seemed as though the one fierce volcano burst had satisfied the need of nature and that the castle and the structure of the hill had sunk again into the void. We were so appalled with the suddenness and the grandeur that we forgot to think of ourselves.

One may perhaps conjecture that, although Stoker had, immediately prior to this, reduced Count Dracula to a pile of dust, he decided against doing the same to his castle—just in case a sequel might be possible. He was, after all, an astute and commercially-minded writer, and indeed he did utilise the vampire theme again in two later books, *The Lady of the Shroud* (1909) and *The Lair of the White Worm* (1911). As many of the subsequent Dracula films have shown, the Master of the Un-Dead can be resurrected from no more than dust, and by the time Stoker had reached this juncture of his story he knew enough about vampires to realise that they were immortal. But that, as I say, is no more than conjecture.

The news that the manuscript had been discovered was first publicly announced in 1984 by its present owner, John McLaughlin, an antiquarian

The vampire Countess (Catherine Mathilde) in the 1981 French film, *The Games of the Countess Dolingen of Gratz*, based on *Dracula's Guest*.

book dealer of The Book Sail in Orange, California. Although it has been available for bids (and there have been unsubstantiated stories of offers ranging from $50,000 to $1 million) it has remained in Mr McLaughlin's possession and there are now plans for a facsimile edition, and for making it the centrepiece of a museum of artefacts relating to fantasy fiction. This would surely be the most suitable home for such an important manuscript.

As I said earlier, however, the discovery of this manuscript has probably created more mysteries than it has solved. *How* did it come to be in America in the first place? *How* could it have remained undiscovered for so long? And, perhaps most importantly of all, *how* did Bram Stoker come to part with what was, after all, the original copy of his most famous work?

At this moment we can only guess—although with a certain amount of conviction.

As Henry Irving's manager, Bram Stoker made several tours with the actor across America: a crucial one in the winter of 1896, and the final one from October 1903 to April 1904. On the first of these he was working on *Dracula* and, by the time of the second, the book was a published success.

Philadelphia was on the Irving tour schedule, and both the actor and his

25

A copy of the vampire story from *The World* newspaper, New York, which was given to Bram Stoker.

VAMPIRES IN NEW ENGLAND.

Dead Bodies Dug Up and Their Hearts Burned to Prevent Disease.

STRANGE SUPERSTITION OF LONG AGO.

The Old Belief Was that Ghostly Monsters Sucked the Blood of Their Living Relatives.

RECENT ethnological research has disclosed something very extraordinary in Rhode Island. It appears that the ancient vampire superstition still survives in that State, and within the last few years many people have been digging up the dead bodies of relatives for the purpose of burning their hearts.

Near Newport scores of such exhumations have been made, the purpose being to prevent the dead from preying upon the living. The belief entertained is that a person who has died of consumption is likely to rise from the grave at night and suck the blood of surviving members of his or her family, thus dooming them to a similar fate.

The discovery ——— —rvival in highly ———ted Ne— —— superstit—

was driven through the chest, and the heart being taken out, was either burned or chopped into small pieces. For in this way only could a vampire be deprived of power to do mischief. In one case a man who was unburied sat up in his coffin, with fresh blood on his lips. The official in charge of the ceremonies held a crucifix before his face and saying, "Do you recognise your Saviour?" chopped the unfortunate's head off. This person presumably had been buried alive in a cataleptic trance.

WERE THEY BURIED ALIVE?

How is the phenomenon to be accounted for? Nobody can say with certainty, but it may be that the fright into which people were thrown by the epidemic had the effect of predisposing nervous persons to catalepsy. In a word, people were buried alive in a condition where the vital functions being suspended, they remained as it were dead for a while. It is a common thing for a cataleptic to bleed at the mouth just before returning to consciousness. According to the popular superstition, the vampire left his or her body in the grave while engaged in nocturnal prowls.

The epidemic prevailed all over southeastern Europe, being at its worst in Hungary and Servia. It is supposed to have originated in Greece, where a belief was entertained to the effect that Latin Christians buried in that country could not decay in their graves, being under the ban of the Greek Church. The cheerful notion was that they got out of their graves at night and pursued the occupation of ghouls. The superstition as to ghouls is very ancient and undoubtedly of Oriental origin. Generally speaking, however, a ghoul is just the opposite of a vampire, being a living person who preys on dead bodies, while a vampire is a dead person that feeds on the blood of the living. If you had your choice, which would you rather be, a vampire or a ghoul?

One of the most familiar of the stories of the Arabian Nights tells of a woman who annoyed her husband very much by refusing food. Nothing more than a few grains of rice would she eat at meals. He discovered that she was in the habit of stealing away from his side in the night, and, following her on one such occasion, he found her engaged in digging up and devouring a corpse.

Among the numerous folk tales about vampires is one relating to a fiend named Dakanavar, who dwelt in a cave in Armenia. He would not permit anybody to penetrate into the mountains of Ulmish Altotem or to count their valleys. Every one who attempted this had in the night the blood sucked by the monster from the soles of his feet until he died.

At last, however, he was outwitted —— cunning fellows. They began to the v——— and when night cam—

manager had several theatrical and literary friends living in Pennsylvania. One of these, to whom Stoker confided his plans for the vampire novel, brought to his attention a newspaper report, 'Vampires In New England', in the New York newspaper *The World*, of February 2, 1896; a copy of this report was later found among his working papers for the book. (See facsimile on these pages.)

It was, I believe, this unknown friend and benefactor who showed more than a passing interest in Stoker's novel and who, when the two men met again during the last Irving tour in 1903–4, was given the manuscript by the author. I also think it possible that Stoker actually used this friend, partly disguised, as the original of the only American character to appear in the novel: the resolute Quincey P. Morris. As readers will recall, it was he who helped in the dogged pursuit of Dracula and was finally in at the kill, driving his bowie knife into the vampire's heart and so causing him to crumble into dust.

Stoker based both his main characters, Dracula and Professor Van Helsing, on real people, so it seems quite feasible that Quincey Morris was also inspired by someone the author had met. And what more generous way could there be to acknowledge a debt than to include that person, albeit disguised, as one of the heroes of the story? Indeed, the portrait of Morris is such a complete and complimentary one that I find it impossible to ignore the feeling that he was a real person.

The descriptions of Morris' clear-cut features and 'brave eyes' thrust him vividly from the page, as does the information that he has 'been to so many places and had such adventures'. The fact that Morris is said to be from Texas rather than Pennsylvania is no more out of keeping than some of Stoker's other ways of covering his tracks; and when the author refers to him as 'a provincial American', this is surely more the terminology one would expect in connection with an Easterner than a man from the vast Southern State.

What adds further weight to this theory is that Quincey Morris is fascinated by stories of vampires—just as Stoker's informant evidently was—and recounts how a vampire bat attacked one of his horses on the Pampas and gorged so much that 'there wasn't enough blood in her to let her stand up, and I had to put a bullet through her as she lay.' He is, of course, also present when Van Helsing relates the history of the Dracula family and is the first to spot the vampire bat flying around Dracula's temporary home at Carfax Abbey. No wonder the Professor says admiringly of him: 'Quincey is all man, God bless him for it.'

All this leads me to the conclusion that the original of Quincey Morris was probably the Pennsylvanian who was so generously given the manuscript of *Dracula* by Stoker in return for his help . . . and who later placed it in a trunk on his farm to gather dust until it was sensationally rediscovered three quarters of a century later.

One question the manuscript has definitely helped us resolve, however, is the actual year in which the adventure of Dracula occurs. Popular opinion has placed it at any time between 1880 and the turn of the century. In fact, as

Stoker's careful use of days and months in his narrative shows, he liked to be very precise about such things.

The manuscript, in its original form, substantiates the year 1887, and when we come to examine the fiction of the story against the reality of certain events taking place in London during the crucial months of September and October in that year, we can see precisely *why* Stoker chose the time in question.

The manuscript also helps us to pin-point the actual site of Count Dracula's house in Piccadilly, a building now as fabled in fantasy literature as Sherlock Holmes' abode in Baker Street. And seemingly just as elusive!

The second page of the Dracula manuscript—containing the text of Stoker's preface—bears a handwritten note of his address: 18, St Leonard's Terrace, Chelsea, London, SW. Today, this smart terrace of houses backing onto King's Road and facing across the open piece of land known as Burtons Court towards the Royal Hospital, and beyond that to the Embankment of the River Thames, has not changed a great deal since the author lived there, between 1890 and the early years of this century. What is *not* widely known is that Stoker began writing the book here in August 1895 and at the same time also made up his mind concerning the crucial London location of Count Dracula's home. This he did while taking the occasional energetic walk from his home to his office at the Lyceum, in the Strand.

Stoker would not have needed long to convince himself, as he strolled along the smart thoroughfare of Piccadilly, resplendent with its Royal Academy, Burlington Arcade, Ritz Hotel and the leafy vista of Green Park—not to mention a number of elegant town houses and apartments at the Hyde Park end—that this would be the ideal place for his nobleman from Transylvania to choose to live.

The number he gives the house in the book is 347, Piccadilly—a deliberately fictitious one, for the numbers do not even reach 300. But the description of the building has the precision of someone writing about a place he has *seen*. To illustrate this point, here are the two vital extracts from Jonathan Harker's diary of October 2, when he is hot on the trail of Dracula. First, he asks the old haulier, Sam Bloxam, to which house in the street he has delivered Dracula's 'nine great boxes'.

'Well, guv'nor, I forgits the number,' the man replies, 'but it was only a few doors from a big white church or somethink of the kind, not long built. It was a dutsy old 'ouse, too, though nothin' to the dustiness of the 'ouse we tooked the bloomin' boxes from.'

Armed with this description, Jonathan Harker has no difficulty in finding the place, as he soon afterwards recounts:

At Piccadilly Circus I discharged my cab and walked westward; beyond the Junior Constitutional I came across the house described, and was satisfied that this was the next of the lairs arranged by Dracula. The house looked as though it had been long untenanted. The windows were encrusted with dust, and the shutters were up. All the framework was black with time, and from the iron the paint had mostly scaled away. It was evident that up to lately there had been a large notice-board in front of the balcony; it had, however, been roughly torn away, the uprights which supported it still remaining. Behind the rails of the balcony I saw there were some loose boards, whose raw edges looked white. I would have given a good deal to have been able to see the notice-board intact, as it would, perhaps, have given some clue to the ownership of the house.

Harker wanders round behind the house and finds some small streets and a couple of mews. He also learns that the notice-board torn from the front of the house had belonged to an estate agent.

Out of interest, I have myself spent several hours walking around this area of Piccadilly, and just as 221B Baker Street has its 'site' where the Abbey National Bank now stands, I believe Dracula's house to have been at 137, Piccadilly, an impressive building now adjoining the Hard Rock Café, and complete with balcony and ironwork, just as Stoker's novel describes it. The property is appropriately occupied by Universal Films, makers of the first *Dracula* film in 1931, and, earlier in this centenary year of the former 'occupier', was refurbished from top to bottom.

I believe I am supported in my view by the fact that the Junior Constitutional to which Stoker refers was a club located at 101, Piccadilly. (By a curious twist of fate, the Arts Council is now situated at 105, Piccadilly.) Furthermore, there are little streets and mews behind the building exactly as Stoker describes them, and in adjacent Down Street is the 'big white church' mentioned by Sam Bloxam: Christ Church.

Turning to the dates of the crucial days in the battle against Dracula, there is interesting circumstantial evidence to be found in the pages of *The Times* of 1887 as to why Stoker fixed on that year. Apart from the fact that the calendar dates fit the year, there were actual events which Stoker found irresistible omens. As the year of Queen Victoria's Jubilee, it was also a focal point of interest.

The novel tells us that Mina and Jonathan Harker first saw Dracula walking down Piccadilly on Thursday, September 22. On that very day, another curious sighting was reported to *The Times* by a Mr Rowland Ward, a fellow of the Zoological Society, living at 166, Piccadilly. Under the heading 'A Shark in Piccadilly', he writes:

Sir, There arrived in Piccadilly this afternoon a fine specimen of the blue shark (*Squalus glaucus*) that was caught by a gentleman, with a line and hook, on the coast of north Cornwall on Wednesday—no doubt much to the surprise of this voracious intruder into the bathing realms of the seaside Britisher, certainly to the amusement of the tourist who captured the 'finny pirate of the ocean'. The shark is only 5 feet in length, but his kind is dreaded by those who 'have their business in the great waters' as much as are his cumbrous brethren. In this jubilee year we have had many remarkable incidents by flood, by fire, by brawls, explosions, and railway calamities; how if the deep were to contribute, so near our homes and among the summer bathers, one of its peculiar touches of trouble, too?

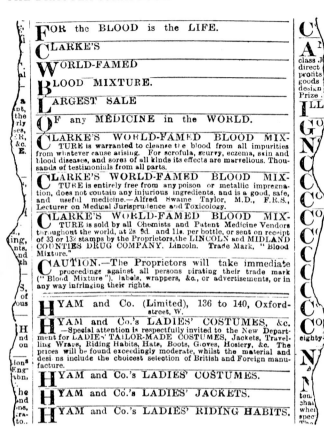

Two of the crucial reports from *The Times* of Monday, October 3, 1887, which helped Bram Stoker fix his time period for the story of Dracula.

Though it is Dracula and not a shark that is seen in Stoker's novel on this date, two other items from *The Times* point towards this being the year the author had in mind.

In London, the city was being swept by a Scarlet Fever epidemic (see facsimile of *The Times*' report), while those Londoners prepared to take a risk against infection had, as the biggest attraction of the day, 'Professor Roche and his Pack of 15 Real Wild Russian Wolves' appearing at the Royal Aquarium. (The only rival to this appears to have been Charles Dickens reading extracts from *David Copperfield* at the Birkbeck Institute in Chancery Lane.)

More telling still, however, was an advertisement prominently displayed for Clarke's World-Famed Blood Mixture, and headlined, 'For the Blood is the Life'. (Again, this is reproduced here.)

If Bram Stoker needed anything more to make up his precise mind, he found it in *The Times* of Monday, October 3—the very day, readers will recall, on which Dracula is confronted in his Piccadilly home and the novel begins to hurtle towards its terrible finale. It was the story of a madman with vampire tendencies. Under the heading of Marlborough Street Police Court, the paper reported:

John Baines was charged with assaulting Annie Cummins with whom he lived. At 11.15 he met her in Piccadilly and said, 'I mean to pay you—you don't mean to come back tonight.' He then struck her on the nose. When she ran away, he pursued her, grabbed her and bit a piece out of her neck. The assault was witnessed by Constable 351A, *John Harker*. [My italics.]

The girl was so injured that she had to attend hospital and would probably be disfigured for life. She appeared in Court with her head enveloped in surgical bandages.

She told the Magistrate, Mr. Mansfield, she was now out of danger from her wound. She said she had kept the prisoner for a fortnight, and during that time he had done no work. He had only recently been discharged from the Army as a dangerous lunatic. He had only left an asylum two months ago.

The Magistrate sent Baines to prison for six months with hard labour.

The parallels between this story and that of the madman Renfield are, of course, obvious, and the evidence for the story taking place is, I believe, overwhelming. My opinion is also shared by several scholars of the Dracula legend, including Professor Leonard Wolf of San Francisco State University, who was born in Vulcan, Rumania, and is the editor of *The Annotated Dracula* (1975).

Stoker was obsessed by time, and in Dracula he uses it to good effect to put his larger theme of Life-in-Death into sharp relief . . . For example, by naming the day on which Mina and Jonathan saw Dracula walking along Piccadilly, he enables us to establish the calendar of events. Dracula's year, clearly, was one in which September 22 was a Thursday.

And that year was 1887!

These, then, are the facts which the remarkable discovery of Bram Stoker's manuscript have enabled us to substantiate. The facts concerning the actual *writing* of the story are equally fascinating, but have been available for rather longer.

3

The Birth of the Legend

The beginning of the Dracula legend in the mind of its creator can be traced to the Yorkshire seaside resort of Whitby—and confirmation of this theory can be found more than 3,000 miles away, on the other side of the Atlantic.

Readers of Bram Stoker's novel will be well aware that it is at Whitby that Count Dracula makes his first landfall in Britain, when he arrives during a violent storm, on board the ship *Demeter*. Because of this, the suspicion has long existed among enthusiasts that it was more than mere chance which made the author settle on this location, and the examination of his working papers in America has at last solved the mystery.

For the simple truth is that Bram Stoker read the name, Dracula, and notes about the vampire tradition of Eastern Europe, in a book which he borrowed while on holiday in Whitby. A magazine article (to which I shall refer later), published just before this visit, may have sparked off his interest in the subject, but in the book he found both the name and the model for his Count.

Piecing together the facts of this remarkable literary creation takes the investigator first to that popular resort straddling the meandering River Esk, and then into the scholarly domain of the Rosenbach Museum and Library in the American industrial city of Philadelphia. In the first place are to be found the settings and words which inspired Stoker's imagination, and in the second, proof positive in the form of a collection of manuscript notes written in the author's own hand.

Driving into Whitby on a bright summer day—on just such a day as that on which the resort is introduced to the reader of *Dracula*—makes thoughts of vampires and the undead seem unlikely, even inappropriate. Yet, motoring along the A171, there is still something a little unnerving about entering the district through Stakesby Vale, and noting hidden in a hollow two small hamlets known as High Stakesby and Low Stakesby.

We cannot know whether Stoker was familiar with these names, for in all probability, when he first stayed in the town in August 1885, he arrived by train via the large resort of Scarborough, some twenty miles down the coast, and thereafter spent his time on Whitby sands or wandering the rugged coastline with its evocative coves like First Nab and The Scar. But he was to grow to love the area for its bracing air and relaxing atmosphere—a haven of tranquillity, in

fact, from the hectic whirl of his life as Sir Henry Irving's theatrical manager in London.

What is beyond dispute is that on a day during that month—perhaps an unexpectedly wet one—he behaved like many another tourist and decided to while away a few hours by reading. And, in the local library in the centre of the town, he came across a book which fired his imagination.

Stoker was a man with an enquiring mind, which perhaps explains why he should have taken down from the shelves an unprepossessing volume which bore the title *An Account of the Principalities of Wallachia and Moldavia, Etc*, written by a certain William Wilkinson who was described as the 'Late British consul resident at Bukorest'. The small book, bound in rather scuffed leather, bore on its spine the date 1820, the imprint of the distinguished London publishers, Longmans, and the library catalogue number 0.1097.

But there was nothing in this external information to prepare Bram Stoker for the information he found as he turned the pages and came to page 19.

That the text *did* immediately interest him is evident from the précis which he carefully made in his scrawling and very distinctive handwriting—and later re-typed—and which now rests in the unique collection of his papers in Philadelphia. It is a curiously exciting and at the same time chilling experience to handle this yellowing sheet of paper and realise that it constitutes, in effect,

Whitby, the picturesque Yorkshire seaside resort where Dracula was 'born'.

Title page of the
hugely influential book
which Bram Stoker
found in Whitby
Public Library.

AN

ACCOUNT

OF

THE PRINCIPALITIES

OF

WALLACHIA AND MOLDAVIA:

WITH

VARIOUS POLITICAL OBSERVATIONS

RELATING TO THEM.

By WILLIAM WILKINSON, ESQ.

LATE BRITISH CONSUL RESIDENT AT BUKOREST.

Dobbiamo considerare queste due provincie, Wallachia e Moldavia a
guisa di due nave in un mar' tempestoso, dove-rare volte si gode la
tranquilita e la calma. DELCHIARO—*Revoluzione di Wallachia.*

LONDON:
PRINTED FOR LONGMAN, HURST, REES, ORME, AND BROWN,
PATERNOSTER-ROW.
1820.

the 'birth certificate' of Count Dracula. I quote in full:

P.19. DRACULA in Wallachian language means DEVIL. Wallachians
were accustomed to give it as a surname to any person who rendered
himself conspicuous by courage, cruel actions or cunning.

The Wallachians joined Hungarians in 1448, and made war on Turkey,
being defeated at the Battle of Cassova in Bulgaria, and finding it

Dracula as conceived by Bram Stoker—a brilliant interpretation based on the original novel, sketched especially for this book by Bruce Wightman, Founder-President of the Dracula Society.

impossible to make a stand against the Turks submitted to annual tribute which they paid until 1460, when Sultan Mahomet II being occupied in completing the conquest of an island in Archipelago gave opportunity of shaking off the yoke.

Their VOIVODE (DRACULA) crossed the Danube and attacked Turkish troops with only momentary success. Mahomet drove him back to Wallachia where he pursued and defeated him. The VOIVODE escaped into Hungary and the Sultan caused his brother Bladus to be received in his place. He made treaty with Bladus binding the Wallachians to perpetual tribute and laid the foundations of that slavery not yet abolished.

On another page in this work, Stoker also found an intriguing footnote about the vampire tradition which was still prevalent in that part of Europe. William Wilkinson obviously considered such peasant superstitions of no consequence in a book such as this, and consequently did not elaborate.

But Bram Stoker, reading the pages more than sixty years later in the Whitby library, made a particular note of this on his sheet of paper. Unconsciously or not, he had found the name of his great anti-hero, although, as I described in the previous chapter, it was his original intention to call the book *The Un-Dead*.

There have, however, been a number of suggestions in biographies of Stoker as to precisely *when* and *how* he began writing the novel. Harry Ludlam, his first biographer, for instance, maintained in *A Biography of Dracula* (1962) that Stoker's son, Noel, told him his father wrote the work as a result of a nightmare about a 'vampire King rising from his tomb to go about his ghastly business' and first put pen to paper 'in 1895 or 1896'.

Daniel Farson, Bram Stoker's grand-nephew, believed that much of the credit for the story should go to a man named Arminius Vambery, a Professor of Oriental Languages at the University of Budapest, who met Stoker in London in April 1890. 'There is good reason,' he has written in *The Man Who Wrote Dracula* (1975), 'to assume that it was the Hungarian professor who told Bram for the first time of the name of Dracula.'

Weight has also been lent to this theory by Raymond T. McNally and Radu Florescue in their book *In Search of Dracula* (1972), in which they write of the meeting, 'The two men dined together and during the course of their conversation, Bram was impressed by the Professor's stories about Dracula "the impaler". After Vambery returned to Budapest, Bram wrote to him requesting more details about the notorious 15th Century Prince and the land he lived in. Transylvania, it seemed, would be an ideal setting for a vampire story.'

Although Vambery certainly appears in Dracula in the guise of 'Professor Arminius', there are no documents in existence today to substantiate this claim. Indeed, in Stoker's own quite fulsome account of his meeting with Vambery there is no mention whatsoever of either Transylvania or vampires— surely the kind of topic a man like Stoker would hardly have failed to mention.

The novel itself appears, from the documents in the Rosenbach collection, to

have been outlined in its basic form in the spring of 1890 . . .

Reading these variously handwritten and typed sheets of paper in the light of the immensity of the Dracula legend today, is both fascinating and salutary. For from this hodge-podge of notes—about the people and places of Eastern Europe, their customs and superstitions; extracts from other works on the supernatural; details about the theory of dreams; even some transcriptions from graveyards—from all this grew a totally unique book. It is rather like travelling down a time tunnel to look over Bram Stoker's shoulder as he painstakingly translates Dracula from an idea to the printed page.

Of all the documents, one dated March 8, 1890, is clearly the most important. For not only is it written in Stoker's unmistakable handwriting, but it contains what is beyond doubt the author's first outline of his projected book.

According to this manuscript, the book Bram Stoker has in mind is to be divided into three sections, the plot to be told in the form of a series of letters from a Count living in Styria to his solicitor in England. There is no reference yet to this strange figure being a vampire—although the author does make a note to himself to 'describe an old dead man made alive, with a waxen colour'.

The three sections of the book are to be: Book I—London, Midsummer; Book II—Tragedy; Book III—Discovery. That Stoker already intended to feature Whitby in the story is evident from two single-line references to the town in the plan for Book II: 'Whitby—argument uncanny things' and 'Whitby—the storm ship arrives.'

Perhaps the most vivid lines in these notes are those referring to another major character, Jonathan Harker. Stoker sketches out almost exactly what is later to become one of the most memorable scenes in the book when he writes, 'Young man goes out—sees girls—one tries to kiss him, not on lips but throat—old Count interferes—rage and fury diabolical—"This man belongs to me"—"I want him a prisoner for a time".'

There are several amendments on these documents in a different-coloured ink, and the indication is that they are of a later date. Of immediate interest

(*Above*) Whitby harbour, where Count Dracula first stepped onto English soil—as it looked in the 1880s.

(*Above, left*) Arminius Vambery, the European scholar and traveller, who is said to have told stories about vampires in Transylvania to Bram Stoker.

37

among these changes are, firstly, the addition of the word Dracula to be the old
Count's name, and, secondly, the deletion of Styria as the setting and the
substitution of Transylvania. Here, thoughtfully, Stoker has written a source
for his information on Transylvania—'Mme Gerard'.

Nor did he need to remind himself of any more, for this was a name with
which he was already familiar. Madame Emily de Laszowska Gerard was a
well-known traveller and historian who for some years had been a contributor
to a London magazine, *The Nineteenth Century*, which had also published some of
his own work. For the July 1885 issue—the one just prior to Stoker's visit to
Whitby—Madame Gerard had written a fascinating essay based on personal
research, 'Transylvanian Superstitions', which was replete with references to
Rumanian peasant customs, vampires and *Drakuluj*—the Devil. Such was the interest in this authentic and ground-breaking article that, three years later,
Madame Gerard incorporated the information in a full-length book, *The Land Beyond the Forest* (1888), which enjoyed a considerable public and critical success.

Knowing that Stoker consulted the writings of this remarkable lady opens up
the possibility that he may have read the magazine article during the month
before his holiday in Whitby and was actually pursuing further information
about vampires when he took down William Wilkinson's book from the library
shelf. Equally, he may only have come to study it, along with Madame Gerard's
more comprehensive book, when he actually began the outline for his proposed
novel in 1890.

Whichever may be the case, Madame Gerard's 'Transylvanian Superstitions' is another important factor in the development of our legend, and I have

38

Dracula in Whitby—a
recent publicity
photograph taken in
the ruins of Whitby
Abbey to promote the
town's association
with the legend.

therefore included an extract from it in Appendix I of this book.

The documents in Philadelphia also reveal one other interesting source of information employed by Stoker: an old coastguard whom he met in the harbour at Whitby, who told him all manner of true stories about the sea and ships. This old salt, whom the most thorough research in Whitby has failed to identify (although he is featured, unnamed, in *Dracula* as 'a funny old man . . . with a face all gnarled and twisted like the bark of a tree'), must similarly be credited as an important inspiration for the novel.

A paper in Stoker's writing dated August 11, 1890, refers to one of several conversations he had with the old coastguard.

'He told me of various wrecks,' Stoker writes. 'There was a Russian schooner of 120 tons from the Black Sea that ran in with all sail. Put out two anchors and she slewed round against the pier. Another ship got into harbour—never knew that all hands were below praying. She was light ballasted with silver sand.'

A further incident related by the coastguard went into *Dracula* almost untouched.

'On 24 October, 1885 the Russian schooner *Dimetry* about 120 tons was sighted off Whitby about 2 p.m. Wind northeast Force 8 (fresh gale) strong sea on coast. Cargo silver sand from mouth of the Danube—ran into harbour by pure chance avoiding the rocks.'

Save for avoiding the rocks, that could be Dracula's ship, the *Demeter*, which, of course, was beached at Whitby on August 7, 1887.

This same coastguard also provided Stoker with some other information which he turned into a short story, 'The Red Stockade', which was published in

America in the September 1894 issue of *Cosmopolitan Magazine*. For some reason it was not published in England, nor was it included in the posthumous collection of his stories, *Dracula's Guest*, which his widow, Florence Stoker, assembled in 1914. It is possible that she did not have a copy of the story since it had never appeared in England.

Whitby itself has acknowledged its association with the legend of the Vampire Count who 'came ashore' there, for the town has opened a museum close to the harbour with the name 'The Dracula Experience'. Undeniably, Bram Stoker owed a debt to the town and its library, and it is a pity that the documents which prove this now rest so far away on the other side of the Atlantic.

Nonetheless, these papers have helped establish, finally, the date and manner in which the idea was born, the inspiration and influences upon the story, and even its location and the name for the central figure. But to discover how Bram Stoker created the actual *character* of Count Dracula we need to look still further back into history.

❧ 4 ❧

The Bloodthirsty Parents of Dracula

The character of Dracula himself is perhaps the most intriguing element of all in Bram Stoker's novel, for he is, in fact, the combination of *two* real historical figures: a pair of bloodthirsty tyrants who are well suited to be considered the 'parents' of the 'King of Vampires'. They are a fifteenth century Prince from the Transylvanian province of Wallachia, commonly called Vlad Dracula, who is reported to have impaled between 23,000 and 100,000 of his enemies; and a sixteenth century Hungarian Countess named Elizabeth Bathory, who, believing that the blood of virgins would provide her with immortality, proceeded to slaughter more than 600 innocent young girls!

It was these two human monsters whom Bram Stoker amalgamated in the creation of Count Dracula—a man who represents himself in the novel as a noble *boyar*, a term applicable in south-eastern Europe only to a nobleman of Wallachia. On other occasions he even boasts of his Szekely—or Hungarian highlander—ancestry, to underline his pedigree. These two important clues lead directly to Vlad and Elizabeth Bathory as the 'infamous originals' of Dracula.

Although I myself have not yet been able to follow the Dracula trail in Rumania, the actor Christopher Lee, famous for his portrayals of the Count on the screen, has done so, and it was he who first told me the stories about this evil couple after he had made a two-month visit to Transylvania in November and December 1971, to film an American documentary for television entitled 'In Search of Dracula'.

'The Dracula of the book is, of course, an old man with white hair and a moustache, who grows steadily younger,' he reminded me, 'and despite his quest for human blood, he is actually a figure of infinite sadness.

'But . . .' he paused for a moment, 'the real Dracula was infinitely worse: a savage, bloodthirsty, psychopathic sadist. And there is surely something much more frightening about a man who *really* lived and did such things.'

The man to whom he refers, Vlad Dracula, was born about the year 1430 in the Transylvanian town of Schassburg. The word *Dracul* in Rumanian means either dragon or devil, and as Vlad was the son of a knight awarded the Order of the Dragon for distinguished military service against the neighbouring Turks, his name actually means nothing more horrifying than 'son of a dragon'. It is only by a quirk of language that it can also mean 'son of the devil'.

The castle of the historic Vlad Dracula in the valley of Arges, Rumania, built by the Impaler in 1460.

Vlad's father, Dracul, was a sworn enemy of the Turks, and as early as 1444 the youngster went on sorties with him over the Danube. In 1448, however, Vlad was captured during one such mission and, as a result of the harsh imprisonment he had to endure, developed a streak of cruelty and disregard for human life that was to colour the rest of his life and cause him to inflict the most terrible punishment on the people of Wallachia, whom he ruled from 1456 to 1462 and then again briefly in 1476, the year of his death. It is said that during his captivity he would amuse himself by capturing mice and rats and then impaling them on tiny stakes in neat rows.

Yet, says Christopher Lee, as far as the people of modern Rumania, which includes the old province of Wallachia, are concerned, Vlad is viewed more as a hero than a villain and is as well known there as Oliver Cromwell in England.

'He is regarded as the defender of Christendom against the Turkish invasions of Europe—a heroic figure despite the fact he was a brutal tyrant. Impaling was his favourite method of execution or torture. It is repellant, repulsive and horrible to think about, but in those days it was fairly common. Vlad would sit down and have his meals while surrounded by people being impaled to their deaths.'

Although his was an age of brutality—among his contemporaries can be numbered Cesare Borgia, Ludovico Sforza, known as 'The Moor', and Louis XI, 'The Spider King'—Vlad outdid them all in his systematic practice of impaling. Indeed, his activities soon grew into a legend which shocked all Europe. One of the earliest accounts was printed by a certain Bartholomeus Gothan in Lübeck, describing in graphic detail the 'many and horrifying deeds of Vlad Dracula—or the Impaler as some call him.'

(*Opposite*) Christopher Lee dressed as Vlad the Impaler while filming *In Search of Dracula* at Bran Castle, November 1971.

42

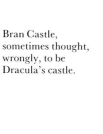

Bran Castle,
sometimes thought,
wrongly, to be
Dracula's castle.

According to this account, Vlad impaled people upside-down, the right way up, even sideways. He arranged the stakes around him in rows or, for variety, in concentric circles. He was quite impartial in those he slaughtered—Bulgars, Hungarians, Germans, Turks, gypsies, Jews and even Rumanians.

On April 2, 1459, for instance, in the city of Brasov in the Carpathians (now a popular ski resort), he cleared a space by burning down a chapel and impaled several thousand Germans, afterwards eating a meal among the blood and screams of the dying. When he noticed one of his own noblemen holding his nose to avoid the stench, Vlad had him impaled, too—but on a taller stake so that he was above the smell!

By 1475, the account continues, Vlad is said to have impaled 100,000 people, almost one-fifth of the population of Wallachia. This puts completely into the shade Robespierre's more notorious Reign of Terror in the French Revolution, for his total was a mere 40,000 souls out of a population of 18 million!

Yet, as scholars have since pointed out, Vlad was *not* a vampire. There is no evidence whatsoever that he ever drank the blood of his victims. So *where* did this element of the fictional Dracula's character originate from?

'It is an interesting jig-saw to fit together,' Christopher Lee told me, 'but not a very difficult one. Stoker, having decided to write his Gothic melodrama about the undead, then decided to combine fact with fiction.

Die facht fich an gar ein grauffein
licße erfcßrőckenlicße ßyftorien, von dem wilden wüt
tricß Dracole weyde Wie er die leür gefpißt ßot vnd
geprüten vñ mit den ßaußtern yn einė keffel gefotten

An early sixteenth century woodcut of Vlad enjoying a meal surrounded by his impaled victims!

'His other books show that he was a bloodthirsty man, so I believe he began to wonder what Transylvanian legend there might be that involved blood. Then he discovered that vampires can live for ever on blood. Vampires can also change themselves into anything, including animals. So what animal lives on blood? Strangely enough . . . the vampire bat. And that, surely, is your jig-saw complete.'

Complete, that is, when we add Countess Elizabeth Bathory, who lived in the remote Carpathian mountains at Castle Csejthe and was a terror perhaps even more unspeakable than Vlad Dracula. A woman of great beauty with a voluptuous, milky-white figure, amber eyes and long raven hair, she well earned the epithet she enjoys today, 'The Hell Cat of the Carpathians'.

'She is, as far as I know, the only proven historical instance of a genuine human vampire who really *did* drink blood and bathe in it to try to retain her youth,' Christopher Lee told me. 'She killed 650 young virgins by torturing and slicing them up in a machine under which she stood and bathed, like someone taking a shower. It is an appalling story but true, and all the documents of her trial still exist. Because she was of royal blood, she was not executed.'

One such document was written by Michael Wagener in Vienna in 1796 and may well have been consulted by Bram Stoker while he was researching in the British Museum, where a copy is still held today. It graphically relates the story

45

The original Bloody
Countess, Elizabeth
Bathory, and her
castle at Csejthe.

of this 'blood-thirsty and blood-sucking Godless woman'.

Elizabeth Bathory was born in 1560 into a family already notorious for its number of lesbians and practitioners of witchcraft. At the age of 14 she was already the mother of an illegitimate child fathered by a peasant boy, but in 1575 she married the Count Ferencz Nadasy to whom she had been betrothed since she was 11. Curiously, Ferencz adopted his wife's maiden name, and both were known as Bathory thereafter. Although Ferencz appears to have been more interested in going off soldiering than in leading a domestic life at Castle Csejthe, Elizabeth did initially try to be a good wife, as Michael Wagener's account tells us:

> Elizabeth was wont to dress well to please her husband and she spent half the day over her toilet. On one occasion, a lady's-maid saw something wrong in her head-dress, and as a recompense for observing it, received such a severe box on the ears that the blood gushed from her nose, and spurted on to her mistress's face. When the blood drops were washed off her face, her skin appeared much more beautiful—whiter and more transparent on the spots where the blood had been.

Elizabeth therefore formed the resolution to bathe her face and her whole body in human blood so as to enhance her beauty. Two old women and a certain Fitzko assisted her in her undertaking. This monster used to

kill the luckless victim, and the old women caught the blood, in which Elizabeth was wont to bathe at the hour of four in the morning. After the bath she appeared more beautiful than before.

Another mysterious figure, described as being 'black-clad with a pale complexion, dark eyes and abnormally sharp teeth', also became a member of this unholy alliance, and the local villagers, who already believed in vampires, were now sure that one—if not a whole pack of them—was living in their midst. When the couple were actually observed one evening with traces of blood around their mouths, the darkest suspicions seemed to be confirmed.

A story even began going the rounds that the stranger was none other than Vlad Dracula himself returned from the grave; but when retribution was later visited on Elizabeth this stranger was nowhere to be found, and it seems more likely that he was just another of her depraved lovers.

Michael Wagener's report concludes:

At last her cruelty became so great that she would attack her victims with her teeth, biting out chunks of their flesh from their necks, cheeks and shoulders. Others she would torture with razors, torches and specially made pincers. When she was ill and could not indulge her cruelty, she even bit those who came near her sick bed as though she were a wild beast.

The vampire Countess, Elizabeth Bathory, who turned from beautiful young woman to hideous old crone, as played by Ingrid Pitt in the film, *Countess Dracula* (1970).

47

She caused, in all, the deaths of 650 girls, some in Csejthe where she had a cellar constructed for the purpose, and others in different localities, for murder and bloodshed became her necessity. When at last the parents of the lost girls could no longer be cajoled, the castle was seized, and the traces of the murders were discovered. Her accomplices were executed, and Elizabeth was imprisoned for life.

Although the story of Countess Bathory can be seen as influential in the Dracula legend, she has also been featured in her own right in three books, *The Bloody Countess* by Valentin Penrose (1962), *The Dracula Myth* by Gabriel Ronay (1972) and *Dracula Was a Woman* by Raymond McNally (1985), as well as a film, *Countess Dracula*, starring Ingrid Pitt (1970), and an excellent BBC radio play, *Vampirella* (1976) by Angela Carter, which featured Anna Massey as the Countess and David March as her 'father', Count Dracula!

Christopher Lee told me that during his two months in Transylvania he visited several of the places associated with Vlad Dracula, including the famous pinnacled Bran Castle towering high on a rock, which he may have visited as a child, and the site of his tomb beside Lake Snagov.

'His tomb is actually on the island monastery at Snagov which is not far from Bucharest,' he said. 'Apparently his body was buried there and his head was cut off and sent to Constantinople. But do you know, the body has *disappeared*!

'I also saw a number of the castles where he stayed, and although some are ruined, one or two are well preserved. Take the castle at Arges, for instance. It

The burial place of Vlad Dracula at the island monastery on Lake Snagov in Rumania. The tomb was recently found to be empty . . .

The astonishing likeness between Vlad Dracula and Christopher Lee revealed by an old woodcut and a profile from the film *In Search of Dracula*.

is a very eerie ruin on top of a gigantic rock about 1,000 feet above a valley. It is almost too good—or too bad!—to be true. The atmosphere, Gothic and brooding, is exactly as Stoker described it, and I was told that students from Bucharest still make bets with each other as to who can stay there for a night.

'I was so fascinated by the place that I brought back some soil as a souvenir. And then in the next vampire picture I made, *Dracula AD 1972*, I threw it onto a grave as my tribute to Bram Stoker's memory.

'But without doubt the biggest surprise I got came when I was shown a wood engraving of Vlad Dracula's face. You'll never believe it . . . but he looked exactly like *me*! It was really quite uncanny. And when someone suggested that maybe it was predetermined I should play *Dracula* I could hardly disagree.' There was the suggestion of a smile on his face as he spoke.

A comparison between the woodcut in question and Christopher Lee as he appeared in the documentary portraying the evil Wallachian Prince (shown on these pages) certainly lends weight to this suggestion!

These, then, are the facts about Dracula's 'parents'. Like all great novels, Bram Stoker's book is a mixture of his vivid imagination combined with research and the skilful mixing of fact and fiction. But perhaps no other writer has ever taken such a pot-pourri of gruesome details and transformed them into

Possibly the success of Dracula during its many years of publication says as much about the tastes of us, its readers, as it does about the remarkable man who created the 'King of Vampires'.

49

5

Dracula by Day— and Other Misconceptions

Then there was the sound of rattling chains and the clanking of massive bolts drawn back. A key was turned with the loud grating noise of long disuse, and the great door swung back. Within stood a tall old man, clean shaven save for a long white moustache, and clad in black from head to foot, without a single speck of colour about him anywhere . . .

This quotation from *Dracula* is perhaps the most striking example of a number of deliberate misconceptions about the vampire Count which the film and stage versions of Bram Stoker's novel have created in the public mind over the years. For in the book, Dracula is actually introduced as an old man who grows younger whenever he feeds on the blood of a victim. Yet, in only a single film—the 1970 Spanish film *El Conde Dracula* (*Count Dracula*), starring Christopher Lee—has the author's original concept been adhered to: everywhere else he is eternally youthful and wears not the slightest trace of a moustache.

There are other, equally striking, elements of the vampire legend which Stoker carefully researched and which have since been carelessly abandoned. Take the Count's supposed fear of sunlight, which makes him seek the sanctuary of his coffin during the day.

In fact, Dracula is several times seen out and about in the daytime—once in the very heart of London, in Piccadilly.

'It was a hot day for autumn,' the heroine Mina Harker narrates in her Journal for September 22, as she and her husband, Jonathan are walking down Piccadilly from Hyde Park Corner. Suddenly, Jonathan spots someone in the crowd—it is Dracula, now grown young since last he was seen.

> Jonathan gazed at a tall, thin man, with a beaky nose and black moustache and pointed beard who was observing a pretty girl. He was looking at her so hard that he did not see either of us, and so I had a good view of him.
>
> His face was not a good face; it was hard, and cruel, and sensual, and his big white teeth, that looked all the whiter because his lips were so red, were pointed like an animal's. Jonathan kept staring at him, till I was afraid he would notice.

No case of mistaken identity there—yet film legend insists that a vampire caught in the sun's rays instantly perishes. What *does* happen is that Dracula's

(*Opposite*) Dracula by daylight—an evocative publicity shot of Christopher Lee!

50

The origin of the legend that sunlight kills vampires—Count Orlok (Max Schreck) dissolving at the climax of the German silent film *Nosferatu* (1922).

powers are severely restricted during the daytime—as Dr Van Helsing explains during his memorable monologue on the undead (once again carefully supported by Bram Stoker's own research).

The power of the vampire, he explains, ceases at the coming of the day. 'Only at certain times can he have limited freedom. If he be not at the place whither he is bound, he can only change himself at noon or at exact sunrise or sunset.'

In fact the concept of the vampire disintegrating in sunlight was introduced with stunning effect in the unauthorised German film version of the novel, *Nosferatu*, made in 1922, and it has remained the film maker's staple ever since.

Then again, Stoker adhered to the old belief that a vampire can only enter a house or building when invited by a member of the household—yet the film Dracula moves everywhere without let or hindrance.

Not surprisingly, one of Dracula's powers which has been considered difficult to portray in films is his ability to crawl head-first down sheer walls.

Early on in the narrative, Jonathan Harker tells us of his host,

My very feelings changed to repulsion and terror when I saw the whole man slowly emerge from the window and begin to crawl down the castle wall over that dreadful abyss, *face down*, with his cloak spreading out around him like great wings.

At first I could not believe my eyes. I thought it was some trick of the moonlight, some weird effect of shadow; but I kept looking, and it could be no delusion. I saw the fingers and toes grasp the corners of the stones,

worn clear of the mortar by the stress of years, and by thus using every projection and inequality move downwards with considerable speed, just as a lizard moves along a wall.

From this description it would appear that Dracula travelled around without shoes! But be that as it may, the paragraph also contains the clue to another popular misrepresentation: here the Count is described as wearing a cloak—yet in every stage and film version of the story he wears evening dress and a long, flowing cape.

The explanation is, once again, easily discovered. The cape plus white tie and tails were actually introduced by the stylish British actor, Hamilton Deane, who produced the very first major stage adaptation of *Dracula* in 1924. Such, indeed, was the impact of this costume upon Deane's audiences, that it has remained identified with Dracula in the public mind ever since. At a stroke, Stoker's concept of the sinister figure, all in black, had to make way for a suave and immaculate man-about-town.

It also tends to be forgotten that Dracula was no mere walking dead man with a lust for blood, as some of the more exploitive films of recent years have suggested. There is more than one attempt by Stoker to win a little of our sympathy for the obsessed, lonely man as well as references to some of his more commonplace accomplishments. For Dracula is not only an excellent butler but an accomplished cook!

Curiously, although Stoker was faithful to vampire lore in so many respects, the idea that Dracula could change into a bat was wholly his own invention. Nowhere in any of the traditional accounts of vampires, gathered from all over

(*Left*) Actor-manager Hamilton Deane who introduced the idea of the cloak-wearing Count Dracula, and (*above*) one of the numerous screen impersonators of the rôle, John Carradine, flourishing his fine cloak in *House of Dracula* (1945).

Dracula's special ability to climb down walls is brilliantly demonstrated by Frank Langella in the 1979 version of *Dracula*.

the world, is there even a suggestion of such a capability. Dracula the bat was a piece of creative imagination which has come to be regarded by many people as the vampire's pre-eminent characteristic.

Stoker also invented the idea that a vampire throws no shadow, as historian Donald Glut has pointed out:

> His reasoning was based on logic. If the vampire can become subtle and intangible, there must be certain non-physical aspects about him. Something that is not physical might not produce a shadow when obstructing the light.
>
> But traditional vampires do possess shadows which throw off sparks in the darkness—another of the seemingly countless traits by which mortals can identify the fiends.

The various film versions are also responsible for encouraging the belief that it takes a wooden stake through the heart to kill a vampire. In fact, Dracula is slain by metal weapons—a kukri which slashes his throat and a bowie knife 'plunged into the heart'. The wooden stake which Van Helsing carries in his vampire hunter's bag is a far more monstrous weapon than has ever been shown on the screen—as this description from the book makes plain:

> The last item was a round, wooden stake, some two and a half or three inches thick and about three feet long. One end of it was hardened by charring in the fire, and was sharpened to a fine point. With this stake came a heavy hammer, such as in households is used in the coal cellar for breaking the lumps.

I suspect, however, that even this fearsome stake and hammer would be powerless to destroy most of the misconceptions which have grown up around Dracula over the years!

'This man belongs to me!' Christopher Lee in the most accurate screen portrayal of Dracula to date—and also his own favourite film—*El Conde Dracula* (*Count Dracula*), made in 1970.

55

🦇 **6** 🦇

The Count Who Won't Lie Down

The 1922 German silent film *Nosferatu*—the very earliest vampire picture—which featured the terrifying Graf Orlok, has become famous as the story that will not die, although, as a blatant plagiarism of Bram Stoker's novel, his widow, Florence, won a court action in 1925 to have it destroyed. Not only have copies of the original movie survived, however, but it has inspired three later versions, a stage presentation and even a musical soundtrack.

It was not just the storyline that the great expressionist director, Friedrich Wilhelm Murnau (1888–1931), lifted and adapted, but the very title, too. For the word *nosferatu*, a Rumanian word meaning 'not dead', occurs in the original novel during a lecture that Van Helsing gives to Arthur Holmwood on the dangers of vampirism.

'Friend Arthur,' he says in his curiously un-English way, as he explains the manner in which vampires propagate their kind, 'if you had met that kiss which you know of before poor Lucy die; or again, last night when you open your arms to her, you would in time, when you had died, have become *nosferatu*, as they call it in Eastern Europe, and would all time make more of those Un-Deads that so have fill us with horror.'

Murnau was one of the first of the silent film-makers to bring horror to the screen, scoring a considerable success in 1920 with *Der Januskopf*, a version of Robert Louis Stevenson's old classic, *Dr Jekyll and Mr Hyde*, in which a small character part was played by a young actor named Bela Lugosi. However, as he scoured the great horror stories for more subjects, Murnau found little that appealed to him among the out of copyright material and set his sights on more recent publications. When he lighted on *Dracula*, he sensed its potential at once.

With his scriptwriter Henrik Galeen, Murnau made a number of changes to the story—but only of the subtlest kind. The Count's name was changed, the major locations were switched from Transylvania to Germany and from London to Bremen, and the time was pushed back to the year 1838; but in essence it was still *Dracula*. For those not familiar with *Nosferatu*, the story may be summarised thus:

> A real estate agent in Bremen sends his recently married clerk, Hutter (Jonathan Harker) to visit a client, Graf Orlok, who, living far away in the Carpathian woods, wants to settle some business affairs. The clerk's journey across these woods—eerie with mist, wolves and strange birds—

(*Opposite*) The first screen Dracula, Max Schreck as Count Orlok, surprised by Gustav von Wagenheim as the Jonathan Harker character, Hutter, in *Nosferatu*, made in 1922.

56

F. W. Murnau, the brilliant German film director, who first illegally filmed Bram Stoker's novel as *Nosferatu*.

proves to be only a mild prelude to the terrors of Orlok's castle.

The day after Hutter arrives he wanders around the deserted rooms and cellars in search of his host and eventually discovers him lying in a sarcophagus—like a corpse with his eyes wide open in a ghastly face. Orlok is a vampire, and vampires must sleep by day.

That night, Orlok approaches the sleeping clerk to suck his blood, but at this very moment the clerk's wife, Ellen (Mina), awakens in Bremen crying out her husband's name. At this, the *nosferatu* draws back from his victim. Hutter has been saved by the telepathic power of love.

The clerk then escapes and sets off for home, pursued by Orlok who now appears more and more like the incarnation of pestilence. Wherever he appears, rats swarm into the streets and people fall dead. He completes the journey on board a sailing vessel (named the *Demeter*, no less!) and, even after the entire crew have died, the ship still continues on its allotted course.

Finally, the vampire arrives in Bremen and is there confronted by Ellen who is determined to save her husband at all costs—even by offering herself. She has sought the aid of a certain Professor Bulwer (Van Helsing) and believes that the evil which Orlok represents can be defeated if faced fearlessly: and so she invites the vampire into her room and allows him to satiate his blood lust upon her. But Orlok neglects to watch the time and, just as he rises from the bed, the first rays of the sun break through the window and he is dissolved into thin air.

Some of the similarities to Stoker's novel will be self-evident from this précis, but the brooding atmosphere, stark images and chilling horror of Murnau's film are unique, and critics have hailed it as the greatest vampire picture ever made. As it was also the first, it certainly set a standard for all those that have followed.

Two major elements undoubtedly contributed to the enormous impact of *Nosferatu*. Firstly, Murnau departed from the usual custom of German film-makers of working in the studios, and shot much of his picture on location in his native Westphalia and on the Baltic coast. The dark hills, thick forests and gloomy skies made an ideal backdrop for the story.

Secondly, he made an inspired choice in the actor to play Graf Orlok, Max Schreck (1879–1937), a stage character actor who, in only his second film rôle, became the original screen vampire—and arguably the most memorable. Schreck (the name, appropriately, means 'terror' or 'fear' in German) created a vampire of absolute frightfulness with his bald head, rat-like face and sharpened teeth, cadaverous eyes and claw-like hands. It was a performance which Lon Chaney, the American 'man of a thousand faces', admired enormously, and which Christopher Lee has called 'the greatest screen interpretation of a vampire'.

Despite such accolades, the picture predictably ran into legal trouble. As soon as she was aware of *Nosferatu*, Florence Stoker went to court and, in July 1925, Murnau was ordered to destroy all negatives and prints of the film.

However, one piece of pirating attracted another: unobtrusively some illegal copies were made, one incomplete version of these helping to sustain the *Nosferatu* legend through occasional screenings in Europe and America.

Then, in 1984, the film as Murnau had originally conceived it was reconstructed following eight years of painstaking work by a long-standing admirer, Enno Patalas of the Munich Film Museum. Starting in 1975, he tracked down six copies of the original film in Switzerland, France and East Germany, and skilfully amalgamated these to complete the story as he believed Murnau had intended.

Apart from the missing captions and the scenes which Patalas reinstated (almost a quarter of the film, making the story-line much easier to follow), he made the startling discovery that the original negative had been tinted: thus making it not only the pioneer vampire movie but also the earliest one in *colour*.

Now it was possible to appreciate that the much criticised scenes of the vampire apparently walking in *daylight* (thereby making his death from the sun's rays quite ludicrous) were, in fact, supposed to be blue-tinted to indicate moonlight. Similarly, a brown tinting had been used for sunlight and yellow for candlelight. Fully restored, it was undeniably an even greater masterpiece than many had thought.

Although this definitive version of *Nosferatu* at last enabled modern critics and enthusiasts fully to understand why Murnau's film had so impressed his contemporaries, the legend of *Nosferatu*—the film that would not die—had begun to grow long before, as far back as 1930, when Murnau himself had helped produce a new version complete with sound.

*   *   *

By a cruel twist of fate, this adaptation of *Nosferatu* was to prove one of Murnau's last ventures as a film-maker. Indeed, the picture which had made his name became, virtually, his epitaph.

The idea for a new version, complete with dialogue and music, came from one of Murnau's disciples, Waldemar Ronger, of Deutsche Film-Produktion, Berlin, who in 1930 proposed extensive editing of the picture and also the renaming of the characters. Ronger felt that there were enough original elements in Henrik Galeen's script to overcome the charges of plagiarism—and in 1930 he won Murnau over to his belief.

Murnau was by then living in Hollywood where he had added to his reputation by making three highly-acclaimed pictures, *Sunrise* (1927), *Four Devils* (1928) and *City Girl* (1930). Together, the two men re-examined all the *Nosferatu* material—including a number of scenes that Murnau had shot and then excluded from the original picture—and restructured the story under the title, *Die Zwölfte Stunde* (*The Twelfth Hour*). The work was begun in Vienna in May 1930 and finally completed in Berlin in November of the same year.

There is still considerable uncertainty as to whether or not Murnau and Ronger shot any new footage for the picture, but certainly they recruited all the

59

actors who had appeared in the 1922 silent version to dub their parts—and in addition Hans Behal to play a Priest who narrates the story. The new names given to the characters were as follows: Max Schreck changed from Graf Orlok to Furst Wolkoff; Hutter, the Jonathan Harker figure (played by Gustav von Wagenheim) became Kundberg; his wife Ellen (Greta Schröder-Matray) was renamed Margitta; and Alexander Granach's Knock/Renfield became Karsten.

In *Die Zwölfte Stunde*, the relationship between Karsten and Furst Wolkoff as servant and master was much more strongly emphasised, while Kundberg played a more central rôle in the eventual outwitting and destruction of the vampire. These elements, plus an added determination on the part of the townspeople to rid themselves of the evil in their midst, gave the story a broader scope than previously.

The introduction of dialogue was strikingly effective and the use of atmospheric music by Georg Fiebiger enhanced the general eeriness of the night scenes. Whether the revised version fully realised Murnau's grand design is doubtful—and certainly when Enno Patalas came to try and recreate the original picture he found it generated more problems than it solved.

As Patalas wrote in the programme for the screening in 1984, 'Methodological problems were caused by the fact that the editors of *Die Zwölfte Stunde* not only recut the film but also added a lot of material, some of which may have been shot by Murnau but not used for the original version.'

Tragically, Murnau was not around long enough after the completion of the new version to resolve such disputes. On March 11, 1931, just a week after the première of his last picture, the exotic South Seas drama *Tabu*, he was killed in a car accident near Monterey. He was just 42 years old.

It was a cruel end to the life of a film-maker of whom Hollywood was expecting still greater things. But his reputation and importance in the industry had already been established with *Nosferatu*—and the influence of the picture still had far to go . . .

*   *   *

The number of film directors who have been influenced by the work of F. W. Murnau is probably impossible to calculate, although the evidence is to be seen in the pictures made over the years by his admirers on both sides of the Atlantic. One such man was the Italian director Corrado Farina, who was so impressed by *Nosferatu* that he decided to remake the story in 1971—but brought up to date as a gangster movie!

Farina, a prolific maker of B pictures, first recalled seeing Murnau's vampire film as a teenager. 'It was shown at a horror film festival in Rome,' he recalled in 1972. 'I'd never seen anything quite so terrifying—not even those terrible photographs from the Second World War of piles of dead soldiers and concentration camp victims.'

When Farina later became a film-maker, specialising in pictures of violence,

Count Orlok about to
spread his reign of
terror: a still from
Murnau's film.

The Count seizing
upon his victim:
another rare still from
Murnau's *Nosferatu*.

the memory of *Nosferatu* was never far from his mind. In 1971 he adapted the basic plot to fit a screenplay in which the criminals became vampires.

The film was called *Hanno Cambiato Faccia* (*They've Changed Faces*) and it centred round the activities of a gangster boss who was a vampire, played by Italy's leading character actor, Adolfo Celi, famous for his earlier rôle as the master criminal Largo, in the James Bond movie, *Thunderball* (1965).

Like his model, Count Orlok, Celi's gangster lived in a grand mansion and orchestrated a reign of terror on the surrounding towns; only the dogged pursuit by a dedicated police officer prevented him from taking total control of the area. But even when the policeman thought he had finally killed the gangster, it was made obvious in the closing frames that the vampire was only faking death. Apparently the production company, Garigliano Films, had their eyes on a sequel if the movie should fare well at the box office—but, it only got a very limited screening outside Italy, despite receiving good notices.

'It was my gesture of appreciation to Murnau,' Farina said later, 'but if all it did was help keep alive the *Nosferatu* legend then I'm happy.'

Even more deeply impressed by Murnau's classic was the controversial young German producer-director, Werner Herzog (b. 1942) who declared in 1978 that *Nosferatu* was 'the most important film in the entire history of the

62

The modern Count
Orlok, Klaus Kinski,
with Isabelle Adjani,
in Werner Herzog's
*Nosferatu—Phantom der
Nacht*, made in 1979.

63

German cinema'—and then proceeded to make his own version of the story.

'I feel pretty close to Murnau,' Herzog explained while working on the picture in the winter of 1978. 'His *Nosferatu* is the most visionary of all German films. It prophesied the rise of Nazism by showing the invasion of Germany by Dracula and his plague-bearing rats in 1922. It also gave a legitimacy to the German cinema that was lost in the Hitler era.

'Besides,' he added, 'the genre of vampire films has not been treated with respect by film-makers for almost 50 years now. Yet this genre is one of the very best soils in which cinema could possibly grow—because it has to do with dreams and nightmares and visions and fears.'

Once Herzog had completed his movie, however, he was quick to insist that it was *not* just a remake of *Nosferatu*.

'My film is an entity unto itself,' he explained in an interview in May 1979. 'It consists of a version absolutely new. The context and the individuals are different. The plot itself is quite a bit changed.

'It is also more than a horror film. Nosferatu is not a monster, but an ambivalent, masterful force for change. His visit to a town almost brings Paradise, for when the plague threatens, the people throw their furniture and their property into the streets—they discard their bourgeois trappings. A new, terrifying kind of freedom comes to them.'

Controversy and an eye for publicity have always been the hallmarks of Herzog's work, and *Nosferatu*, with its million-dollar budget, the eccentric Polish-born actor, Klaus Kinski, in the lead rôle, and the beautiful French actress, Isabelle Adjani, as Lucy, was no exception. Perhaps, however, the event which generated most headlines was his plan to release thousands of rats into the narrow cobbled streets of the thirteenth century town of Delft in Holland, to illustrate the plague which Nosferatu unleashes on the town.

On his arrival, Herzog went to some pains to assure the press that the film crew were not coming as 'an invading army'—but that they might 'cause some inconvenience once in a while'. However, when word got out about his plans to use rats, tremors of apprehension began to spread through the ancient town.

'My film is about a community that is invaded by fear,' he explained in an attempt to assuage the unease he sensed building up. 'The rats are a very decisive element, almost a key to the film because they signify this invasion of fear.

'We are using laboratory rats from Hungary,' he went on. 'They are albinos with red eyes and very beautiful. Very beautiful—and very scary! They are also quite small and distinct from savage rats; they are tame, and will be sterilised so they cannot reproduce. We only want to release them in controllable places, like very narrow streets. We will block all the escape routes; we will close the doors; we will build a fence. Not one single rat in the whole world can escape!'

However, as the newspaper stories which followed this pronouncement graphically reveal, Herzog's optimism was not fulfilled.

A total of 11,000 rats were bred in Hungary for the scenes, and then imported to the barn of a local farmer where they were to be kept until required. On

Film-maker Werner
Herzog releases
thousands of rats into
the streets of the Dutch
city of Delft while
filming *Nosferatu* in
1979.

seeing them, however, Herzog was not satisfied with their appearance and had
them all painted grey.

To help supervise what was undoubtedly going to be a complex manoeuvre,
the film-maker hired Holland's leading rat expert, a biologist named Martin T.
Hart. But all around him opposition continued to grow—fuelled by the fact
that the canals of Delft had for years been the breeding grounds for huge rats
and the problem had only recently been brought under control.

The result was that, despite the co-operation Herzog had been promised, he
found all manner of obstacles being put in the way of his crucial scenes.
Afterwards, he described the eventual outcome.

'They really held us to ransom,' he said. 'We paid some people to look after
the rats until we needed them. When we came to get them for filming, the
keepers wouldn't hand them over. They demanded three times the original
price, claiming they had fed the rats on sugar and bananas every day. So some
of my crew raided the place at night and there was a running battle—blood
everywhere! But we got the rats back.'

Even so, Herzog was still faced with the local *burgemeester*'s refusal to grant
permission for the rats to be freed in the streets.

'I had to resort to a stratagem,' he explained. 'I pretended to pack up and
leave Delft—but before anyone could stop me I suddenly released the rats and
shot the scenes. A lot of them ran away, I'm afraid. We never found them.'

Herzog's determination to make a superlative vampire picture was only
matched by that of his star, Klaus Kinski, the multi-talented but unpredictable
actor, born in 1926, who first made his living reading poetry in a highly

65

individualistic style, before turning to films—with stops on the way as an army deserter, a prisoner of war, a mental patient and a worker with prostitutes and thieves, as he happily admits.

'Until Werner Herzog called me at two o'clock in the morning to ask me to play the part I had never thought about Dracula before,' he says today. 'Or only briefly, like a cloud passing through my mind. But from the minute he talked to me about it I felt the vampire growing inside me.'

Kinski's gruelling experiences both in making the picture, and in studying the vampire legend in literature and on film, have made his comments on the subject particularly interesting.

'Everybody is fascinated by vampires,' he says. 'It has to do with our unconscious feelings about physical desire as much as psychic things. To be bitten—it's very physical, very erotic. The desire to be blood-sucked is actually very natural.

'When I was a child I used to love fairy tales because there you can let your imagination go, there are no limits, they free your fantasy. This is what happens with the story of Dracula, and this psychic part of our lives is very powerful.

'People are released from the day-to-day prison of their lives when they come to a film like *Nosferatu*, but it is difficult to define the reasons *why*. Creation itself is a mystery. It is good that not everything can be explained.

'If Dracula was only the figment of someone's imagination, he is still real. It is important that people can connect a visual image with an imagined one. As an actor, I am only a vehicle for ideas. But I think this is the first serious film on the subject that has been made in the last 50 years.'

Kinski says that Werner Herzog never gave him specific instructions on how to play Nosferatu, although he did not come to the film entirely unprepared. In 1970 he had appeared in *El Conde Dracula*, Jess Franco's very faithful version of the Bram Stoker novel with Christopher Lee in the title rôle. Kinski had played Renfield with what most critics described as 'extreme restraint' and an evident insight into a tortured mind. Speaking of the rôle at the time, he revealed that he himself had once been locked in a madhouse for ninety days and had found the experience a traumatic as well as fascinating one.

'The only thing Werner insisted on for Nosferatu was the rat-like ears,' Kinski says of the picture. 'He was mad about the ears! Otherwise I thought it all up myself—the bald head, the long nails and the teeth placed centrally in the mouth. We had them like that because there is no animal who sucks blood with fangs wide apart. I know it looks like Murnau's *Nosferatu*, but I had never seen that film before we made ours.'

Kinski spent hours every morning preparing for the rôle, using special white Japanese Kabuki make-up which is absorbed into the skin, in order to achieve his walking-dead appearance.

'My make-up alone took five hours in the chair each day,' he recalls, 'and two hours before that I had to shave my head and put on special cream. It was my decision to be bald. I thought Dracula was something that was not human, but not a monster either.'

66

Kinski's painstakingly-wrought performance earned him glowing praise from the critics.

'His vampire is the epitome of suffering,' said Mike Bygrave of *The Observer*. 'This is a Dracula we're meant to feel sorry for despite his grotesque appearance. His doom is to walk the world with all the emotions, the longing for love of an ordinary man, yet to be cut off from mankind and unable to fulfil his longing. It's a physically remarkable performance. Kinski's body seems to move with the weight of centuries on his back.'

Derek Malcolm of *The Guardian* also underlined this view when he wrote, 'In the part Kinski seems like a man who wishes to be dead but cannot be, a sad and frightened as well as frightening figure. It is a physical performance that will be difficult to follow, moulded with an intensity that's as startling as that of Bela Lugosi.'

And even the horror film fan magazine, *Famous Monsters*, chipped in: 'A new classic has been created—a monument for the memory of Murnau and a hallmark for Herzog.'

*   *   *

Apart from these direct tributes to Murnau's original classic, extracts from the film have also been featured in other pictures.

In 1945, for instance, a number of scenes were included in a semi-documentary about vampires produced by the French director, Jean Painlève, entitled *Le Vampire*. Then, in 1962, a much-edited version of the movie was

Another still from Klaus Kinski's magnificent interpretation of the vampire Count Orlok in *Nosferatu*.

67

shown in a half-hour American television series, 'Silents Please'.

This *Nosferatu* dropped all references to Renfield and Van Helsing, but the Count and all the remaining characters had their original names restored. In a nicely apposite twist of fate, the picture was retitled simply *Dracula*, and the new credits boasted that the story was 'based on the famous horror novel by Bram Stoker'!

In 1965, an 8mm home movie version of this television presentation was put on sale by Entertainment Films who, seemingly unhappy with the title (or perhaps to cash in on the popularity of Christopher Lee's 1958 *Horror of Dracula* which was then on re-release yet again!) called the film *Terror of Dracula*.

Some seven years later, Blackhawk Films released both the 'Silents Please' TV abridgement as *Dracula*, and an almost complete version of Murnau's silent original with his title, *Nosferatu, The Vampire*.

In 1970, Spanish film-maker Pedro Portabella included some footage in his picture, *Vampir*, a tribute to the tradition of the vampire. The movie concentrated largely on the shooting of the Christopher Lee picture, *El Conde Dracula*, which was made in Spain around Barcelona.

Talking about this film, Christopher told me recently, 'It was Portabella's personal presentation in film form of his impressions about the vampire in the cinema only. It was shot in black and white and is very strange in many respects. I mean, it shows me arriving on location before I'm made up—and then actually playing in the picture. I didn't even know half the time they were shooting!'

Nonetheless, *Vampir*—which also includes extracts from the Bela Lugosi films and from Carl Dreyer's 1932 picture, *Vampyr*, based on the Joseph Sheridan Le Fanu story, 'Carmilla'—was screened at the Metropolitan Museum of Modern Art, though it has not yet been shown on general release.

In 1973, an American film called *Casual Relations*, made by Mark Rappaport, featured an extract from the picture as well as a satire on vampire films called 'A Vampire's Love', starring Mel Austin.

Nosferatu has been shown a number of times on television in several countries, while many of its scenes have been used in film programmes to illustrate both Murnau's skill as a director and also the picture's influence on later vampire films.

It was in 1981, however, that its influence spread still further with the presentation at the Stratford East Theatre in London of a ballet entitled *Nosferatu*. Staged by the English Dance Company, it retained a considerable amount of Stoker's original story-line, to which were added dance steps and the music of Poulenc's Organ Concerto, Strauss's Zarathustra and extracts from *Peer Gynt* and *Carmina Burana*.

John Percival of *The Times*—who had the misfortune to attend on the night when the ballerina playing Mina was unable to dance because of injury and was instead replaced by a vampire hunter!—was nonetheless impressed by the 'rather entertaining' ballet, as he wrote in his review of February 4, 1981:

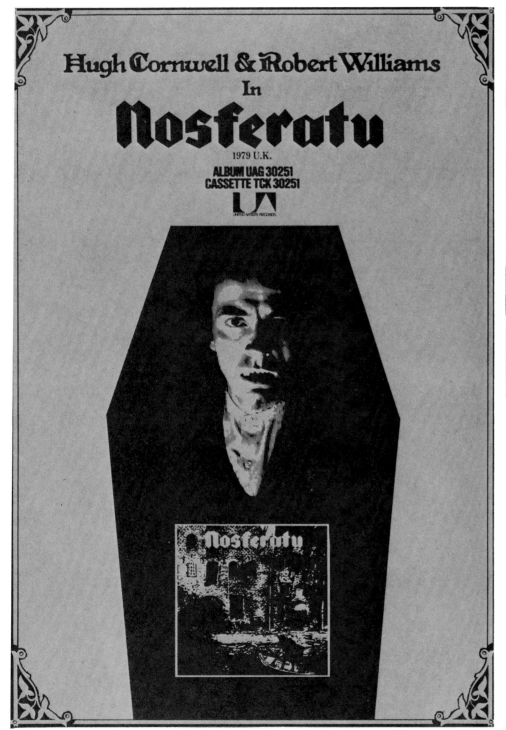

Nosferatu old and new—a poster for the original 1922 movie and a leaflet for the 1979 record.

Ross McKim is able to switch from self-disgust to courtly charm as the undead hero, and his menaces are as convincing as his comic moments. At the moment of death, you almost expect to see his clenched hand, raised in the spotlight, change into fleshless bones, just as in the movies.

It seemed odd to have his attendant spirits at one point enticing honest Jonathan with crosses, but Sue Little makes a notably pale and interesting Lucy, who becomes a lot less bloodless when Nosferatu starts to court her in a wittily impassioned duet. She and McKim are joint choreographers of the ballet, but I suspect that each took charge of certain scenes rather than trying to do everything between them. Their different temperaments seem to make a good match.

What Bram Stoker might have thought of his tale as a ballet one can only conjecture—although, as a theatre lover by inclination and profession, he would probably have watched with interest, if not amusement. Murnau, ever the experimenter, would doubtless have approved.

Both men would, I suspect, have enjoyed the latest manifestation of the legend, a long-playing record made by Hugh Cornwell, the vocalist and guitarist of 'The Stranglers', and Robert Williams, formerly with the famous American musician, Frank Zappa. Called simply, 'Nosferatu', the album has grown out of the two musicians' admiration for the vampire legend, and it is amusingly subtitled, 'a musical soundtrack to a film that will never be made'.

'Rhythmic Itch', which starts the record, is a moving tribute to Dracula, while in 'White Room' the Un-Dead reminisces over his past life and unrequited loves. The title track, 'Nosferatu', is the most frenzied of the album and moves at a terrific pace as the hunted Count is chased through the streets with dawn approaching . . .

The record has been widely admired by rock fans as well as by critics, one of whom wrote recently, 'Hugh set out to create a "work of fear" and has achieved his ghoul (*sic*). Nosferatu simply has to be heard to be (dis)believed.'

Nosferatu is now as much a part of the Dracula legend as the original novel itself. Indeed, I believe the influence of F. W. Murnau's creation may in time extend as far as Bram Stoker's tale has done. What a fate for a piece of plagiarism!

Count Orlok, like his *alter ego*, Dracula, will surely never die!

7

Playing the Master of the Undead

The actor most universally associated with the character of Dracula is, without doubt, Bela Lugosi, whose life and career became literally overtaken by the image of the vampire count which he created in the late nineteen twenties. Yet the fact is that, although Lugosi enacted the part of Bram Stoker's Dracula for several years on the stage, he only twice played the Count on the screen. To be sure, he was cast as a vampire in other cinema productions and the character he portrayed was little different from that of his original interpretation—but the remarkable truth remains that one of the most enduring horror reputations of this century was built on the most slender evidence.

Born Bela Blasko, the son of a Hungarian banker, in Lugos on October 20, 1882—a mere five years before that dramatic year in the life of Stoker's master of the undead—Lugosi created his archetypal image for the stage version of *Dracula* produced on Broadway in 1927. Based on the novel and adapted by Hamilton Deane and John L. Balderston, the production ran for twelve months in New York and then had two hugely successful years touring America.

The play was to prove the beginning of an association from which Lugosi could never extricate himself, whether he might want to or not, and which was mainly responsible for his eventual decline into a morass of financial and marital problems and drug addiction. Undoubtedly the vampire image absorbed even his personal life, for not only did he take to giving interviews while lying in a coffin, but after his death, on August 15, 1956, he was buried—according to his instructions—wearing his Dracula cape. It was a tragic and rather pathetic end for a man whose contribution to the horror genre should not be underestimated, and whose presence off screen could be as unnerving as on it.

As a film-struck youngster I saw him in London, during his visit to England in April 1951, to begin yet another tour of the 'Dracula' stage play. Although I only saw him briefly, when he arrived on April 10, the memory of his dark, brooding features and that slow, heavy, unmistakable Hungarian accent, remain as indelibly fixed in my consciousness as his portrayal of the Count on the screen. My one disappointment was that I did not get his autograph, signed—appropriately—in blood-red ink, but I do have a collection of now somewhat brown and faded press cuttings of his visit, which form a treasured part of my Dracula memorabilia. They provide graphic proof that Lugosi was

able to attract the kind of idolisation from his fans that only the super-stars of today can match.

He was accompanied on the trip to England by his fourth wife, Lillian, and was clearly in an expansive mood, for he talked at some length to journalists about his connections with the story of Dracula and how it had earned him the epithet 'the aristocrat of evil'. Although he patiently answered predictable questions from the more sensation-seeking newspapers about his love of raw steaks and blood oranges, he was serious when asked about his life and career.

'I was not a very brave child while I was growing up in Hungary,' he confessed. 'I grew up in Transylvania where the legend of Dracula comes from and never did I go down into our cellar. It was full of bats!

'I wanted to become an actor right from being a child, though, and I was very fortunate in being able to get a place at the Budapest Academy of Theatrical Arts. There is only one place in the world where it is worthwhile to be an actor—Hungary. For there you have a four-year training course and once you have passed through that you have nothing to worry about. Even in your old age you still get a pension. In America and the rest of the world there is always the fear of unemployment.'

From 1901 he was a member of the Hungarian Royal National Theatre, and played many leading rôles, including Hamlet and a number of romantic leads. He then became active in politics and organised an actors' union; but with the collapse of the Austro-Hungarian empire in 1918 and the establishment of a republican regime, he fled to Germany.

'I left my country in 1920 and have never been back,' he said with a note of sadness in his voice. 'I do not like to live under a dictatorship of any kind and I am now an American citizen.'

It was in Germany that Lugosi made his first films—and also came into contact with Dracula for the first time. His reputation as an actor had secured him an introduction to the expressionist director, F. W. Murnau, and, as we have seen, a small part in the film *Der Januskopf*.

'It was one of the first true horror films,' Lugosi recalled. 'But to someone like me, who had concentrated on drama and romance, it was just another part. I

(*Opposite*) A rare portrait of Bela Lugosi as he appeared as Count Dracula on the Broadway stage in 1930.

Bela Lugosi out of his Dracula costume, photographed in his Hollywood home in 1939 with wife Lillian and son Bela jnr.

played a few more small rôles in German films before emigrating to America the following year.

'What I didn't know then was that Murnau was planning to film Bram Stoker's book and call it *Nosferatu*. I don't suppose I would have got the part if I had stayed in Germany, but one can never tell . . .

'I first read *Dracula* in Germany and it made quite an impression on me. Although it is a fanciful tale of a fictional character, it is actually a story which has many essential elements of truth. I was born and reared in almost the exact location of the story, and I came to know that what is looked upon merely as a superstition of ignorant people, is really based on facts which are literally hair-raising in their strangeness—but which are *true*.

'I know that many people have left the theatre after seeing *Dracula* with a sniff at the fantastic character of the story; but many others who think more deeply have gained an insight into one of the most remarkable facts of human existence. *Dracula* is a story which has always had a powerful effect on the emotions of an audience.'

Lugosi said that from the time he read Dracula he dreamed of the day when he might have the chance to create the rôle.

'When I first came to Broadway I was still playing romantic parts—the Spanish lover in *The Red Puppy* and the Valentino-type sheik in *Arabesque*. Then in 1927 the New York stage producer Horace Liveright acquired the rights to the play and began looking for someone to play Dracula.

'In America, you know, they have the type system of casting. And there was no male vampire type in existence. Someone suggested an actor of the Continental school who could play any type, and mentioned me. It was a complete change from the usual romantic characters I was playing, but it was a success—*such* a success!

'Now that I have played the rôle of Dracula on the stage and screen for almost a quarter of a century, people often ask me if I still retain my interest in the character. The answer is, I do—intensely.

'You see, because many people regard the story of Dracula as a glorified superstition, the actor who plays the rôle is constantly engaged in a battle of wits with the audience in a sense, since he is constantly striving to make the character so real that they will believe in it.'

The success of Dracula on stage quickly branded Lugosi as a 'horror specialist', so he was not unduly surprised when, four years (and a thousand performances) later, he was called to Hollywood to recreate the rôle in the planned Universal Pictures movie based on the play. It was adapted and directed by Tod Browning, the circus performer turned film-maker who had been responsible for some of Lon Chaney's best screen performances.

What Lugosi did not know at that time was that he had not been first choice for the rôle. Browning himself had wanted to star Chaney, but the 'man of a thousand faces' had died the previous year. Also on the short-list were: character actor Paul Muni; Ian Keith, a specialist in villainous rôles in costume spectaculars; and Conrad Veidt, the star of the German expressionist classic,

74

The Cabinet of Dr Caligari (1919). It would have been a strange twist of fate if Veidt had secured the rôle, for he and Lugosi had appeared together in Murnau's *Der Januskopf.*

Tod Browning, the brilliant Hollywood director who made the classic 1931 version of *Dracula* with Bela Lugosi.

As it was, Bela Lugosi flung on the Count's cloak and, slicking back his dark hair and whitening his features, became the archetypal Count Dracula. He did, though, acknowledge his debt to Tod Browning in making his performance as effective as it was.

'On the stage the actor's success depends wholly on himself. He goes onto the stage and gives his performance in what to him seems the most effective manner. But in the studio the responsibility is shifted to the director, who controls the actor's every move, every inflection, every expression.

'In playing in the picture I found that there was a great deal that I had to unlearn. In the theatre I was playing not only to the spectators in the front rows but also to those in the last row of the gallery, and there was some exaggeration in everything I did, not only in the tonal pitch of my voice but in the changes of facial expression which accompanied various lines or situations. I "took it big", as the saying is.

'But for the screen, in which the actor's distance from every member of the audience is equal only to his distance from the lens of the camera, I have found that a great deal of repression was an absolute necessity. Tod Browning continually had to "hold me down".

'In my other screen rôles I did not seem to have this difficulty, but having played Dracula a thousand times on the stage—in this one rôle I found that I had become thoroughly settled in the technique of the stage and not the screen. But thanks to director Browning I unlearned fast.' Bela Lugosi expanded further on his attitude to playing Dracula in a rare personal article, 'I Like Playing Dracula' which was published in *Film Weekly* in July 1935 and is reprinted at the end of this book.

The screen rôle of Dracula was long behind Lugosi when he came to Britain in 1951, but he gave an enthralling description of the way he prepared himself to play the Count on stage.

'It takes me about half an hour to warm up before the curtain rises,' he said. 'I never eat a meal before a performance—I like to go on thirsting for blood! I really have to get myself in the mood. I don't like to be spoken to for an hour before each show, and even for half an hour after we've finished I'm *still* Dracula.'

He also explained that the style of performance had changed over the years. 'It is now played perfectly straight and has been modernised since I first took it on the American stage. You see, horror is not what it used to be.

'When *Dracula* was first presented on Broadway there were members of all audiences who took it literally. People screamed and fainted. The first aid staff were kept busy all the time. I did not dare to pretend to bite my victims' necks for fear of a hysterical reaction from the public. Nowadays the customers— even the children—know it all. They have seen plenty of horror films. But we believe there is still a demand for an old-fashioned spine-tingling horror

play—and always will be as long as it is properly presented.'

Lugosi was doubtless gratified by the critical response to his British tour. The reporter from the *News Chronicle* summed up the consensus of opinion in these words: 'This is melodrama in the Henry Irving tradition, magnificent, macabre and gloriously blood-curdling; not staged, but invoked, and declaimed rather than acted. Hollywood could never provide realism like this.'

Lugosi was also asked by the English reporters if he ever scared his wife or his son, Bela jnr.—to which he replied with a smile, 'How could I? They see me in my underwear and how can a man have any dignity in his underwear?'

Today this statement reads like a rather sad comment on his career after *Dracula*. For though the picture made him a star of the cinema, it doomed him to playing only horror parts, and his stylised form of acting further restricted the rôles he could play. As critic Donald F. Glut has put it, 'In the minds of the motion picture executives he was eternally the Count Dracula of 1931, and he was condemned to continue enacting virtually the same performance in numerous films that were to follow . . . He also made perhaps the greatest mistake of his life when he turned down the rôle of the Monster in *Frankenstein* (1931). The Englishman Boris Karloff accepted the part instead and, being a far better actor than Lugosi, nosed the Hungarian performer into second-place status.'

The only other occasion when Lugosi played the *real* Count Dracula on film was in 1948, in a picture called *Abbott and Costello Meet Frankenstein*, also made by Universal, in which he appeared with the two popular American film comedians, Bud Abbott and Lou Costello, in a farcical tale which managed to introduce just about every kind of monster, from Frankenstein's Creature to the Wolf Man and, of course, Count Dracula.

Coming to the part-proper again after almost two decades, Lugosi wisely played the vampire Count with more restraint, and his chalk-white make-up and dark lips made him seem even more sinister. Although newspaper critics found the combination of two comedians and the various figures of fright quite

(*Opposite*) Another dramatic moment from *Dracula* with Lugosi and Dwight Frye who played the madman, Renfield.

Bela Lugosi as the Count in the comedy film, *Abbott and Costello Meet Frankenstein* (1948).

77

ludicrous, the film was stylishly directed by Charles Lamont and has been described by some fans as 'the best spoof of the horror genre ever made'.

Certainly, *Abbott and Costello Meet Frankenstein* contains one of Lugosi's best performances, apart from the original Dracula. As for the other movies in which he appeared as a vampire—usually taking up no more than a few minutes and demanding nothing more of him than to rise from a coffin and wearily frighten some unsuspecting victim—it is perhaps kindest to draw a veil over them. All that remains to be said is that, despite all his disappointments and the decline in his career, Lugosi never lost his affection for the real Dracula, and apparently nursed a desire to the end of his days to remake the Bram Stoker novel in colour and 3D!

Bela Lugosi's great achievement was to bring the first real Dracula to the screen and to create an image which will never be forgotten. All his successors have been matched against it, right from the man who first took over his mantle.

*   *   *

John Carradine, the lean and hungry-looking actor who inherited the mantle of Dracula from Bela Lugosi, had, like his predecessor, turned down the offer from Universal Pictures to play the monster in *Frankenstein*, because the part had no dialogue. In 1945, however, when he was offered the rôle of Dracula in Universal's *House of Frankenstein*, co-starring with Boris Karloff, he accepted with alacrity. Not only was Karloff an old friend, but, as so often during his rumbustuous life, he needed the fee!

According to John Carradine, Bela Lugosi turned down the chance to return as Dracula in this film because he had grown tired of being identified with the rôle. It seems more likely, however, that he was under contract to other studios at this time. Whichever is the case, Carradine gave a memorable portrayal as the vampire Count, which was immediately acclaimed as being much closer to Stoker's original conception. As James Robert Parish and Michael R. Pitts wrote in their essay on the actor in the magazine, *Focus on Film* (Summer, 1973):

> Some consider his screen portrayal of the Count to be the most definitive on celluloid. His austere features, penetrating eyes and resonant voice combined to make him the archetype of the Count as written by Bram Stoker, and an evil contrast to the more theatrical Bela Lugosi or the later suavity of Christopher Lee. In later years, Carradine would play Dracula on the stage, replete with moustache, just as Stoker had described him.

Despite the fact that John Carradine has appeared in the astonishing number of over 400 films and is known as 'The Thin Monster' and a 'VIP of Villany' among horror film fans, as an actor he holds a unique distinction, being described by some as one of the most outrageous ham actors, and by others as one of the greatest contemporary performers. Whichever is true, he has rarely been out of work in a career which now spans more than half a century.

John was born Richmond Reed Carradine, on February 5, 1906, in Green-

Boris Karloff drawing a stake from John Carradine in *House of Frankenstein* (1944).

One of John Carradine's later interpretations of Dracula, complete with top hat and cravat!

wich, New York, the son of a noted newspaperman and attorney. He came to public attention at the tender age of 14 when he delivered an essay denouncing the League of Nations, and then, after quarrelling with his parents, left home to become an itinerant painter. In 1925 he gave up this precarious existence for the even more precarious one of the stage.

Following two years in small stock companies, he hitch-hiked to Hollywood in the hope of finding more lucrative work in films. While waiting for parts, he appeared at the Vine Street Theatre in Los Angeles and there formed what was to become a life-long friendship with another struggling young actor, Boris Karloff. Both were destined to become kings of horror—but Karloff, of course, got a start on his friend by accepting the offer of Frankenstein.

In 1934, however, Carradine himself entered the world of horror movies with a small rôle in *The Black Cat* which starred Karloff and the already disenchanted Bela Lugosi. It was the first of several pictures the two men were to make together, and Carradine recalls the Hungarian actor with affection.

'Oh, he was a charming man. He always had a bucket of red wine on the set, which he pulled out gracefully all day long. He never forgot his lines and never lost his affability. He was a very affable man.'

More horror rôles followed in the next decade—including the highly rated *The Mummy's Ghost* for Universal in 1944—as well as work on the stage, where he honed his art as a fine Shakespearian actor. Then, in 1944, came the Dracula rôles, first in *House of Frankenstein* and its sequel, *House of Dracula* (1945). He has explained his reasons for so dramatically changing his interpretation of the part from that of Bela Lugosi:

'When they asked me to do it I said, "Well, I'll do it if you let me make him up something like the way he is described in the novel—with the white hair, the long, white moustache and the hawk nose." And they let me do it to a certain extent. But I certainly didn't want to play him with the same black pompadour that Bela had. And at that time I hadn't done the play. I've done it since.'

It was while he was touring with the play of Dracula in the late 1950s that he explained how he created his very distinctive appearance.

'I devised it from the description given in the book by Bram Stoker. I had read *Dracula* as a boy in my early teens, but I went through it again to be sure my recollections of the Count were correct before I did anything.

'The aquiline nose is made of a plastic material cast from a plaster mould made on my life mask. I thought this would be easier to apply than nose putty and wouldn't melt under the heat of the lights like gelatin. At first, though, I had trouble putting make-up on the nose because it slid off, so I had to coat it with spirit gum before applying the greasepaint. The nose also had a tendency to turn chalky white and had to be darkened between acts.

'The sideburns I swept up like spiked horns and coloured them to match the moustache and greasepaint. I used small thin red lines to make my eyes look large and the pupils dilated, and I blacked my eyebrows with greasepaint and powder to stick on the false eyebrows at 45 degrees.'

A highlight of John Carradine's stage performance as Dracula was a very realistic-looking final scene in which a stake was driven into him as he lay in his coffin. Although he would immediately rise to take his curtain calls, audiences were still often taken aback by this gruesome *finale*.

'Actually,' John Carradine explained later, 'they just stuck it in my armpit— they couldn't afford too much realism!'

His irrepressible humour helped him to win over one audience in Detroit when all the props refused to work and he kept hearing little chuckles coming from all over the auditorium. As he came out to take his final bow, he hissed at the rows of patrons:

'If I'm alive, what am I doing here? On the other hand, if I'm dead, why do I have to wee-wee?'

It was a line perhaps even more memorable than Van Helsing's original last warning—and he used it regularly thereafter.

At this time—September 1957—John Carradine became the first actor to play Dracula on television, in a special production for the 'Matinee Theatre' series presented by NBC. It was a performance very similar to that given on the stage, but with a wider range of sets.

His later appearances as Dracula in films were, sadly, of a much inferior kind. In 1966 he appeared in the absurdly titled *Billy The Kid v Dracula*, directed by William Beaudine, a veteran Western film-maker. The picture brought the vampire to the Old West where, after drinking the blood of a number of victims, he was finally staked by Billy the Kid with a surgeon's scalpel!

Carradine, who sported a satanic moustache and beard and a bright red neckerchief, declared of the picture some years later, 'Easily my worst film. I needed the money, to be honest; actors have to live, too, you know. It was a bad film. I don't even remember it. I was absolutely numb.'

The most unlikely Dracula film of all? John Carradine with Chuck Courtney in *Billy the Kid Versus Dracula*, made in 1966.

He also remembers little about *Las Vampiras* (*The Vampire Girls*) which was made in Mexico, directed by Federico Curiel, in 1967. 'It was just another one I did quickly. I was working with Spanish-speaking actors though I spoke English. It was very difficult to figure out what the hell was going on!'

Two years later, in 1969, he starred in *Blood of Dracula's Castle*, directed by producer Al Adamson, in which, for the first time, he did not play the vampire Count, but his murderous butler, George, who sacrifices young girls to the moon! Two other proposed vampire films in which it was announced he was to appear, *Dracula v the Beasts of Zarcon* and *The House of Dracula's Daughter*, scheduled for 1972 and 1973 respectively, were, perhaps thankfully, never made.

Despite the undoubted decline in the standard of the later Dracula pictures which John Carradine made, his contribution to the legend, in terms of the authentic look he brought to the character, should not be forgotten. Indeed, in America there are those who believe he was the best screen Dracula. Not long ago, the *Saturday Evening Post* carried a tribute to him entitled 'A Sentimental Journey to Dracula's Home Town', describing his still active life in Oxnard, California. The author, Gene Smith, wrote:

Unlike most people I have never considered Bela Lugosi's interpretation of Dracula to be the equal of that of John Carradine. You will note that when Lugosi bends over the victim, a fiendish delight illuminates his features, whereas, on the other hand, with Carradine there is a look of infinite sadness to the gesture.

Carradine does not drink the blood because he wants to; he drinks it because he must. I think this is a clue to the character of the Un-Dead. When at last he does in fact die the final death over at Borgo Pass near his castle, with the great steel stake driven through his heart, a look of great peace and quietude comes into his features. This shows that he knows, has known through 600 terrible, haunted years, that he is accursed and that now, at last, his soul will find peace.

Certainly Bram Stoker's character entered a new phase in his screen development through the work of John Carradine. And overlapping the latter part of his career, another actor, across the Atlantic, was also bringing a new dimension to the master of the un-dead. His name—like that of Bela Lugosi—has become synonymous with Dracula: Christopher Lee.

*   *   *

The Dracula who leaped onto the screens of Britain and then the rest of the world in the late 1950s was again a very different vampire from Bela Lugosi's reserved and impeccable mid-European Count. The makers of this new film, Hammer Films, knew that public tastes had changed in the twenty-five years since the appearance of the Universal Dracula and now the public thirst was for . . . blood! Lashings of it, in gruesome technicolor!

By yet another curious twist of fate, the man who was to play this new Dracula came to the part after a notable appearance as the monster in

Christopher Lee makes his impressive début as the Count in Hammer Films' Dracula (1958).

Although Christopher Lee has always refused to make a burlesque of the Dracula story, he is a man of good humour—as this off-set picture taken in 1965 reveals.

Hammer's *The Curse of Frankenstein* (1957)—the very rôle Lugosi had so scornfully refused to take after his success as the master of the un-dead.

Time has shown that the casting of Christopher Lee as the Dracula of the 'sixties and early 'seventies was an inspired choice, though, like Bela Lugosi, he has become rather more closely identified with the part than he would like, being an actor of considerable range and with many more rôles to his credit than those of his horror movies. Yet when any discussion of Bram Stoker's novel on the screen takes place, his name will invariably feature largely in it.

I have known Christopher for some years (having co-authored a book with him, *Christopher Lee's New Chamber of Horrors*, in 1974), and I have spent many pleasant and interesting hours discussing films with him in his London flat in a square where, incidentally, Boris Karloff was a neighbour for some years. He is as tall (six foot four inches) and commanding a figure in real life as he appears on the screen, and his background is almost as distinguished as that of the Count from Transylvania.

Christopher was born on May 27, 1927, the son of a career soldier who commanded the King's Royal Rifles and was a friend of Edward VII. On his mother's side he can claim descent from the infamous Borgia family, and an early childhood memory is of meeting Prince Yusupoff, the man who assassinated Rasputin.

Christopher received a classical education at Wellington School, and then served in the RAF in Yugoslavia during World War II, doing intelligence work and a little espionage. After the liberation of Germany, he visited a number of the concentration camps, including Dachau, a deeply disturbing experience which, he says, provided him with such a close-up view of the charnel house side of real life that he is unaffected by anything he sees or does on the screen.

He went into acting in 1947 through a chance introduction and, after a number of small character parts, foisted on him mainly because of his height and foreign appearance, he drew attention in the *Frankenstein* movie, and then became a star in what was to prove a whole series of Dracula pictures for Hammer.

Christopher started off full of enthusiasm for the rôle, but as the stories became progressively more ludicrous and moved ever further away from Stoker's concept, disillusionment set in. Today, although he still admires Bram Stoker's book—and indeed is an expert on supernatural literature in general—he has no desire to play the Count again. With one exception: *if* a film were to be made that exactly followed the story as told in the book.

The success of the first of the movies, *The Horror of Dracula* (1958)—sometimes known simply as *Dracula*—was out of all proportion to Hammer's original expectations. It had a budget of just £81,413, of which the writer, Jimmy Sangster, received £1,000, the cast £7,310, and the crowd scenes cost a total of £87! The shooting schedule was six weeks.

Christopher had not seen either the Lugosi or Carradine versions of Dracula when he made the picture, although he read the book carefully and determined to make the Count a more dynamic and also more human figure than his predecessors.

'Dracula is a great rôle and a very difficult one to play properly,' he told me. 'I found it a very stimulating challenge to make him convincing to today's cynical, worldly audiences. I saw him as aloof, dignified and austere, exploding into tigerish activity when necessary.

'When I was making *The Horror of Dracula* I tried to remain true to the book—but otherwise it was entirely personal. What came onto the screen was a combination of my knowledge of Stoker and trying to invest the character with dignity and nobility, ferocity and sadness. I introduced things like Dracula's walk, the way he spoke, the look of him and also his movements.

'I have always tried to invest the part with human elements, because I believe audiences are more shocked by a sad vampire than a mad one. I put the sadness into the rôle because there is a terrible sadness about him. He doesn't want to live, but he's got to. He doesn't want to go on existing as the un-dead, but he has no choice. I have even tried to show that Dracula sometimes regrets his blood-drinking habits.'

Christopher Lee's appearance as Dracula was also different from that of his predecessors. A wig of thick grey hair with a widow's peak and combed straight back created the illusion of pointed ears. And, for the first time on the screen, his Dracula had red eyes and long canine teeth.

He told me he had no particular problems with the specially made teeth which fitted over his own: he could talk easily enough, but not eat. 'Dracula's not really such a peculiar looking character in that respect is he?' he said. 'After all, I've seen plenty of people with teeth almost as long as his—I expect many people have.'

The red eyes were quite a different matter. 'They were terrible to wear,' he recalls, 'very painful and uncomfortable. They used to make me cry and I could only see hazily when I had them in. The coloured part didn't actually cover the pupils of my eyes so I didn't actually see red, but it was still difficult to see when I was charging about.'

Although blood and gore was very much the order of the day in the Hammer Dracula pictures, Christopher was able to refrain from actually having to bite his victims.

'I nuzzled them all—never kissed them on the lips,' he said. 'Then I masked what followed. I believe it is more effective that way. Some people have said the raised cloak suggested a bat.'

In the movies he also spoke rapidly and with total self-assurance, though never for long. 'In the book Dracula hardly ever stops talking,' he explained. 'I think in the films he should only speak when he has something to say. I used to cut a lot of my lines and leave only things that were short and to the point: phrases like, "You have failed me. You must be punished!"'

Christopher Lee's attention to detail and integrity when playing the rôle made *The Horror of Dracula* a financial and critical success—as well as establishing him as a star. But he did not rush into an immediate sequel. However, the following year, 1959, he was invited to star as Dracula in an Italian spoof of horror films, *Tempi Duri Per I Vampiri* (*Hard Times for Vampires*). But unlike his predecessor, Bela Lugosi, he refused to make fun of the rôle into which he had just breathed new life.

'It was supposed to be a gag, but I didn't want to be Dracula,' he recalls. 'The idea was that I played opposite Italy's top comedian of the time, Renato Rascel, as an unnamed vampire called the Baron. I suppose I couldn't help looking a little like Dracula, but there were some subtle differences that I insisted on to prevent the part from being too much of a resemblance.'

Lee did not, in fact, play the Count again until 1965, when Hammer made *Dracula—Prince of Darkness*. (They had, however, made a film in 1960 entitled *Brides of Dracula*, which was rather misleading because there was no Count Dracula, only a blond-haired 'disciple' called Baron Meinster, played by David Peel.) In this second picture, he worked with his favourite co-star, Barbara Shelley, though he was not happy at having to wear his red contact lenses all the time.

'I thought that was a mistake,' he says. 'Dracula's eyes should only turn red for two reasons. Firstly, if he is furious, or else if he is about to take blood.'

Actual filming was also made arduous because of the closing scenes in which Dracula falls through the ice of a castle moat and drowns. This involved some complex shooting and a very damp spell in the water! (A special sequence of photographs of this scene is included in these pages.)

This second performance undoubtedly established Christopher Lee as *the* modern Count Dracula, but the quality of the series went downhill thereafter.

85

One more 'death' for Dracula! A remarkable sequence of photographs of Christopher Lee's watery end in *Dracula, Prince of Darkness* (1965). In the picture immediately to the left he is seen being given directions by Terence Fisher before filming of this sequence commenced.

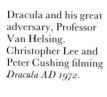
Dracula and his great
adversary, Professor
Van Helsing.
Christopher Lee and
Peter Cushing filming
Dracula AD 1972.

In 1968 Hammer made *Dracula has Risen from the Grave*, a title which did not please Lee, and once again making the film provided him with problems.

'Dracula's return was a very unpleasant scene for me to do,' he recalls. 'A trickle of blood had to run into my tomb of ice and this meant lying fully clothed in water for hours.'

Then there was a scene when he had to wrench a wooden stake out of his chest.

'That was *all* wrong,' he says. 'Everyone knows a stake through the heart is the very end of a vampire. I objected at the time, but I was over-ruled. It ended up as an extremely gruesome sequence with blood pouring everywhere.'

The finale was very similar in theme. 'I had to stagger around impaled on a crucifix like a fly on a pin,' he says. 'Then a look of sadness crossed my face. Blood came out of my eyes and mouth, and finally I disintegrated into a pool of blood covered by my cloak. Stirring stuff photographically—but not the kind of thing to satisfy a skilled actor!'

Despite Christopher Lee's growing reservations about the films, Dracula was now unquestionably a box office winner for Hammer and the following year, 1969, they starred him again in *Taste the Blood of Dracula*. At the conclusion of shooting, the star announced to the press that he was not going to play the part again . . .

However, an offer the next year to appear in a Spanish/Italian/English/West German co-production, *El Conde Dracula* (*Count Dracula*), which was announced as a faithful representation of Stoker's novel, made him change his mind. And indeed this movie, produced by Harry Alan Towers and directed by Jess Franco, remains his favourite to date.

'The script was pretty dismal,' he recalls, 'but the character of the Count was right: an old man in a black frock coat, with white hair and a white moustache, getting progressively younger during the story as he gets stronger from the blood of his victims. The make-up was correct, the clothes were correct. I didn't have the pointed nails or the hair on the palms of my hands because these were details that could never be picked up. But that apart, it is the only time that Stoker's character has been presented authentically on the screen.'

Before that year was out, Lee had also made another Dracula for Hammer, *Scars of Dracula*, in which he made a valiant attempt to reinstate some of the elements from the Stoker novel which the earlier screenplays had jettisoned—including the Count scaling the walls of his castle like some giant human lizard. He was not altogether unhappy with the result.

Two years later, Hammer decided to break completely new ground by transferring the vampire Count from his traditional Victorian setting and bring him into the modern day, in a film announced initially as *Dracula Today* but actually released as *Dracula AD 1972*.

Christopher made no bones about his feelings. 'I think it's totally wrong to take the story out of its historical period,' he said. 'But in a weird way it quite works.'

Once again he played Dracula with the same mixture of dignity and humanity that he always brought to the rôle, and he even managed to get inserted into the script a line direct from the novel, in which the Count challenges Van Helsing: 'You would play your brains against mine . . . against *me* who has commanded nations!'

Christopher told me why he had done this. 'It was my way of paying a tribute to Bram Stoker to show him that, as far as I was concerned, his original characterisation was still very much alive to me. People who knew the book immediately got what I was doing. It was a desperate cry from my heart to the author that at least I was trying to get something original into the film!'

When, in 1973, *Dracula is Dead . . . and Well and Living in London* was announced, Christopher told the press that not only was he making the picture very reluctantly, but that it would be his last.

'I'm doing it under protest,' he said tersely. 'I think it is fatuous. I can think of twenty adjectives—fatuous, pointless, absurd. It's not a comedy, but it's got a comic title. I don't see the point.'

Later, he expanded on his feelings. 'I don't believe people like to see Dracula made fun of. They take him seriously. They may laugh at some of the things in the picture, but they never laugh *at* him.

'It seems to me the film-makers are getting further and further away from the original concept of the character, which I believe is totally wrong. People say to me, "Well, then, why go on?" My answer is that as an actor I have to make a living. And there are millions of people all over the world who want to see me play the part. In whatever context I play Dracula I don't change. I remain the same. I just hope people realise that I am struggling against insuperable odds to remain faithful to the author's original character.'

Christopher described the Dracula he was asked to play as 'a mixture between Howard Hughes and Dr No', and his dislike was not tempered by

Hammer's decision to change the title of the film when it was released to *The Satanic Rites of Dracula*.

There was little more joy for him in 1977 when he appeared in the humour-tinged French production, *Dracula Père et Fils*; nor in the following year's *Count Dracula and his Vampire Bride*, made in America.

Since then, however, the tall, forbidding actor has been kept busy working in Hollywood and television and has no plans to return again as Dracula. Unless, and until, a serious attempt to put the original novel on the screen is made.

'I have no intention of playing the character again because I'm disenchanted with the way he has been presented,' he told me at one of our more recent meetings. 'Bram Stoker's book has never been done in its entirety on the screen. They have simply been writing stories into which they fit the character, and that just doesn't work.

'Dracula is a superb book and it deserves to be done properly, but the trouble is, that would cost an enormous amount of money. There'd have to be shipwrecks, craggy mountains, many varied locations, special effects and so on. So far only bits and pieces of Stoker's book have been presented on the screen.

'If I was offered Stoker's story *exactly* as he had written it, I would do it again—and *that* would be for the very last time.'

Whether or not Christopher's dream is ever fulfilled, his contribution to the legend is assured—although it is easy to understand why he wishes it did not swamp so much of his other excellent screen work. Others have learnt from his example—and that of Bela Lugosi and John Carradine—and to date no other actor has allowed himself to become quite so identified with the rôle, although several have taken up the vampire's black mantle . . .

* * *

In 1973, the same year in which Christopher Lee's *The Satanic Rites of Dracula* was released, the first feature-length television version of *Dracula* was produced by director Dan Curtis. A seasoned admirer of the original novel, Curtis hoped to make the definitive Dracula but in the end had to confine his story mainly to an English setting. What *was* a triumph for his picture was the casting of famous screen 'bad guy' Jack Palance as the Count.

Born on February 18, 1919, the son of a Pennsylvanian coal miner, Palance brought an element of restrained violence to the screen that had not been seen in any previous portrayal. Despite his gaunt, tight-skinned look—the result of plastic surgery necessitated by the severe burns he received in World War II, when the bomber plane he was piloting crashed—Palance can play anguished and soulful parts with great skill, and this is precisely what he brought to Dan Curtis' production.

'I had a pretty good idea of what other actors had made of Dracula,' Palance said while filming in England in 1973, 'but it seemed to me that here was a man scarred inside by a curse that he could never lift, though he managed to hide it except when his need for blood was absolutely overwhelming. Then he would

take what he must have by the sheer magnetism of his personality. And he did it with style, too.'

Style has been a strong feature of Jack Palance's acting career, and he has twice been nominated for Oscars—in *Sudden Fear* (1952) and *Shane* (1953). As a former professional boxer, he also gave a memorable performance in *Requiem for a Heavyweight* on American television.

He was attracted to Dan Curtis' production of *Dracula* by Richard Matheson's excellent script, which managed to keep the atmosphere of the original in those sections of the novel which it retained. Much of the action, in fact, concentrated on Dracula in England and the country house where he takes up residence. His next-door neighbour is the beautiful Lucy Westenra and, by the force of his personality, he successfully turns her into a vampire. But retribution comes at the hands of the dogged Dr Van Helsing who finally corners him in a sunlit room and stakes him to his own dining-room table.

Co-starring with Palance were a trio of fine British actors: Fiona Lewis as Lucy, Simon Ward as Arthur Holmwood and Nigel Davenport as Van Helsing. The production has been seen on both sides of the Atlantic and was praised by one critic as being 'like a vampire's bite—deep and penetrating.'

Jack Palance, the famous Hollywood tough guy, gave a memorable performance in the 1973 version of *Dracula*.

*   *   *

Another first for the legend at that time was *Blacula* (1972), an ingenious variation of the story starring the noted black Shakespearian actor, William Marshall. In America there was an ever-expanding market for films starring

91

Nigel Davenport as
Van Helsing and
Simon Ward as Arthur
keeping Jack Palance
at bay in Dan Curtis'
1973 movie version of
the novel.

black performers, and with hindsight it seems inevitable that the timeless story
of the master of vampires would sooner or later lend itself to such an
adaptation.

William Marshall, a towering figure of six foot five inches, with a magnificent
deep voice, was an ideal actor to play the part of Prince Mamuwalde, an
African nobleman who visits Count Dracula in Transylvania and is turned into
a vampire. Then, after lying entombed for 150 years, he is revived in present-
day Los Angeles and sets about satiating his blood lust.

Marshall, who was born in Gary, Indiana, on August 19, 1924, came to the
picture with an impressive list of credits to his name on both the stage and in
films—not to mention the intriguing fact that in 1950 he had been understudy
to Boris Karloff when the great man was playing Captain Hook in 'Peter Pan'!
Writing to me about the film shortly after he had completed shooting, he said:

Blacula is the first classic vampire film to be written for Black central
characters. The premise of the story is provocative and the characterisation of the central figure—in the writing of which I was invited to
participate—is unusual and interesting. An African spokesman, Prince
Mamuwalde, arrives in Europe in 1815 with his bride, on a mission of
protest against the renewal of the slave trade following the invention of the

92

The first black
Dracula—William
Marshall who has
starred in two pictures
as Blacula.

cotton gin. The Prince's tour of Europe brings him to the Balkans, and one night he and his wife attend a dinner at the Castle of Count Dracula. That's when all his problems begin . . .

Marshall had got in touch with me concerning a long-playing record he wanted to make from one of my earlier books, *Vampires at Midnight* (1970), and it gave me the opportunity to discuss his unique approach to the Dracula legend.

'I knew very little about vampires before I became involved in this project,' he said. 'So I took a crash course in Dracula, reading the book and looking at some of the earlier films. I also talked to people about *why* audiences are still so responsive to the story after all these years.

'Perhaps most important of all as an actor, I had to know about vampires from the vampire's point of view. And not just any vampire: how would an African Prince of the early nineteenth century feel about being taken captive in Transylvania and doomed to live out eternity hungering for human blood?

'What I learned I put into the film. And perhaps the most interesting thing I discovered was that an effective vampire movie must be flooded with urgent emotions of anguish, yearning, terror and, ultimately, relief.'

Marshall worked hard on both the script and the actual filming, and he recalls one unusual incident which helped him resolve the question as to why the Dracula story is so durable.

'We were shooting a street scene in Los Angeles one night, when a very beautiful woman wearing a long black cape approached me. She introduced herself and then startled me by saying that she wanted to be a vampire!

'"Why?" was all I could weakly think of replying, my mind mostly on the scene I was about to play. Her eyes lit up at this. "Because vampires live forever!" she exclaimed. "There's really no way to kill them. If you pull the stake out of their hearts, they revive. They can't really be hurt, no matter what happens."

William Marshall and Vonette McGee in the 1972 black vampire movie, *Blacula*.

'I turned away from her not knowing what to say. But I've never forgotten her words.'

William Marshall's reward for his dedication to the project was to see his rôle as Blacula critically acclaimed, earning him two major fantasy awards, including one from the Count Dracula Society in California which called the movie, 'the most horrifying film of the decade'. The picture also took more money at the box office for its makers, American-International, than any other movie they had ever made. A sequel was inevitable.

The provisional title for the second Blacula was *The Name is Blacula*, but to William Marshall's dismay it was changed to *Scream, Blacula, Scream*. The story had the black vampire resurrected by a voodoo cult to launch another reign of terror in the streets of Los Angeles. This time, however, his marauding was brought to an end in a novel way, through the destruction of a doll made in his likeness: a traditional voodoo rite.

Sadly, this film failed to match the success of its predecessor, a fact which William Marshall puts down to a weak script.

'I would still like to play Blacula again, though,' he told me. 'I think he has been proved a legitimate heir to Dracula and certainly there are a lot of possibilities to be explored with his character. So I'm keeping my stakes crossed!'

*   *   *

The most recent actor to don the Count's black cloak has been the darkly handsome Frank Langella—once described as 'the greatest sex symbol since Tyrone Power'—who starred in director John Badham's *Dracula*, filmed in 1979. At the time of its release, *Time* magazine referred to it as 'the expensive *Dracula* that the gang at Hammer Films must have dreamed of making back in the '50s and '60s.' And yet the truth is that the movie—made, appropriately, by Universal Pictures who began the whole cycle back in the 'thirties—has only served to show that the definitive Dracula *still* remains to be made . . .

Certainly Langella, the son of a New Jersey businessman who was born on January 1, 1940, came to the film with the advantage of having played Dracula for two years in an award-winning New York production. His knowledge of the Count was therefore considerable.

'It was an enormously difficult rôle for me to play,' he confessed later. 'I didn't begin to grasp Dracula until I was close to opening in the play in Boston for the previews. Then I finally began to understand him through his *humour*.

'One day in rehearsal I couldn't get the first act, when Dracula enters and is introduced to Van Helsing and the other characters. I suddenly thought to myself, how would I feel if I'd been lying in a box all day and, when I got up, there was an invitation to dinner with two pretty girls, the doctor who lived next door and a young lawyer? I would be rather delighted because I had something to do, and also because it would be fun to toy with these mere mortals. When that sense of pleasure in what he was came to me, other things began to develop

95

and he became a man who seduced his victims rather than attacked them.

'I also came to the conclusion that there was an aspect of the Count that had never been fully explored before—his vulnerability, his sensitivity, his fear. I've always felt that he's the kind of man, if he has lived for 500 years and experienced different times and different cultures and different peoples, who's bound to have gained a certain amount of philosophy about life, so that he doesn't spend all of his time lurking and looking for blood. He needs blood to survive, but when he gets it, he has another ten or twelve waking hours to pass. He can enjoy the company of other people, he can find himself more attracted to one woman than another, it doesn't have to be purely indiscriminate blood-letting.

'What I had to find was a key to what would make him work today. I decided he was a highly vulnerable and erotic man—not cool and detached and with no sense of humour and humanity. I didn't want him to appear stilted, stentorian or authoritarian as he was so often presented. I wanted to show a man who was evil, but lonely and who could fall in love.

'Dracula knows what his problem is and he doesn't make excuses about it to women. He doesn't ask whether he can have their blood. He says, "I'm going to drink it—because I need it".

'It also turned out, when I started talking to women before I played the part, that they all saw Dracula in a very sexual way. When I came to do the love scene there was an audible swooning and sighing from the women in the audience at every performance!'

It is evident from these remarks that Langella had formed his own very special view of the Count for his stage adaptation—and indeed the play was warmly received by the critics, including the *New York Times* pundit, Clive Barnes who wrote, 'Frank Langella is one of our few great actors.' The show also impressed the man who was to produce the movie, Walter Mirisch.

'I truly had no idea what to expect when I went to the theatre,' he said. 'But he had created a completely different character, one with charm, sex appeal and, most important of all, he endeared himself to the audiences. I decided right then to make the film.'

Director John Badham felt the same. 'Langella makes Dracula sexy, fascinating, and therefore dangerous. Evil doesn't have to be repulsive.

'I don't mind saying he's the only American actor in years who can play with style, who can wear capes, who can carry it off. It's tough to get away with that sort of thing.'

Indeed, Langella did find making the picture—shot primarily on location in England—tough going; although not quite for the reasons he expected.

'I'd performed the part 400 times on the stage by the time we began filming and I found it was getting through to me, affecting the way I lived,' he explains. 'For instance, after a while I started wondering why I couldn't walk through walls! Then, one day, I was stuck in a traffic jam, and I started day-dreaming that I could just elevate myself like Dracula and transport myself to where I wanted to go.

(*Opposite*) 'The sexiest Dracula of them all'— Frank Langella and Kate Nelligan in John Badham's *Dracula* (1979).

96

'It was all a bit worrying. And if I had been younger I might *really* have got caught up in it all. After all, we're all caught up in the Dracula myth in a way, we're all interested in the dark side of ourselves which he represents. I just had to keep reminding myself that I was an actor playing a rôle.'

In creating what one newspaper called 'the sexiest Dracula of them all', Langella had to fight hard *not* to have to wear the traditional pair of fangs.

'Nobody is frightened by fangs,' he explained later. 'It has been done too many times. When I was offered the part the first thing I said to the producer was, "No fangs". But he kept trying to persuade me to wear them. I held out and I think I was right. Dracula is now more effective and perhaps more frightening.'

True or not, the high hopes of Langella and Universal for this *Dracula* were not to be realised. Despite a huge budget—four million pounds, which ran to six million—and co-stars such as Laurence Olivier as Dr Van Helsing, Kate Nelligan as Lucy and Donald Pleasance as her doctor father, the picture was not well received either critically or at the box office.

American critic Richard Schickel spoke for many people when he wrote, 'It was as if someone decreed that this was to be a *Dracula* for adults—forgetting that the story has always been for adults regressing into adolescence, with its hopeless loves and wild fantasies. There is no point in retelling this tale if you are going to be stuffy about it.'

Not surprisingly, plans for a sequel—made possible by a deliberately open ending—were quietly shelved. And it was left to the *Daily Mail*'s critic, Quentin Falk, to write the epitaph on the movie when it was shown on British television in May 1983.

Pound for pound—or should it be pint for bloody pint?—the 1979 film version of *Dracula* has probably been the least successful in 50 years of transplanting the Transylvanian count to the screen. It cost more than £6 million and was a resounding box office flop . . . counted out by cinema audiences less than a year later—leaving the likes of Bela Lugosi and Christopher Lee to lie easy in their successful caped incarnations.

So it would seem that the challenge of bringing Bram Stoker's *Dracula* to the screen exactly as he wrote it—and just as Lugosi and Lee have dreamt of doing it—still remains. For as *Time* magazine has commented, 'One reason Dracula remains forever undead is that no amount of cinematic miscalculation can entirely loosen his grip on our imaginations.'

8

Tales of the Vampire Hunter

Dr Van Helsing, the 'Vampire Hunter' and Count Dracula's redoubtable adversary, is not just one of the great protagonists of the novel—as important to the story as, say, Professor Moriarty is to the legend of Sherlock Holmes—but also very much the man Bram Stoker would like to have been. It would be wrong to imagine that the author was not satisfied with his real occupation as manager to Sir Henry Irving, but Van Helsing was undoubtedly his *alter ego*.

The good doctor long ago achieved immortality in the pages of the book, but more recently he has also done so on the screen, where three actors in particular have helped make him as famous as the Count himself: the American, Edward Van Sloan, who first impersonated him; Peter Cushing, who has played him more times than anyone else and become widely associated with the rôle; and Lord Olivier, certainly the most famous man ever to have played the part.

Bram Stoker's admiration for Van Helsing is evident in every line of his description of the story's shrewd and courageous hero.

> He was a man of medium height, strongly built, with his shoulders set back over a broad, deep chest and a neck well balanced on the trunk as the head is on the neck. The poise of the head strikes one at once as indicative of thought and power; the head is noble, well-sized, broad and large behind the ears. The face, clean-shaven, shows a hard, square chin, a large, resolute, mobile mouth, a good-sized nose, rather straight, but with quick, sensitive nostrils that seem to broaden as the big, bushy brows come down and the mouth tightens. The forehead is broad and fine, rising at first almost straight and then sloping back above two bumps or ridges wide apart; such a forehead that the reddish hair cannot possibly tumble over it, but falls naturally back and to the sides. Big, dark blue eyes are set widely apart, and are quick and tender or stern with the man's moods.

This is an identikit portrait of the author himself—an 'amiable, red-haired giant with deep blue eyes', to quote the description Stoker's wife, Florence, once gave of him. Like Stoker, Van Helsing's Christian name is Abraham and he has an eye for the women. The two men also share an interest in white magic and sorcery, as Stoker's later book, *Famous Imposters* (1910), with its detailed study of magicians and practitioners of witchcraft, bears witness.

Dr Van Helsing's peculiarly foreign style of speech is, however, very different

(*Above*) Bram Stoker who saw himself as the Vampire Hunter, Professor Van Helsing, and (*below*) Edward Van Sloan who first portrayed the character on stage and screen.

from Stoker's gentle Irish burr, and we have no evidence that the author was interested in medicine with anything other than a layman's natural curiosity about health—although when writing about the various emergencies with which the doctor was faced, such as performing a trephining operation, or giving a blood transfusion, he did, as we have seen, seek expert advice. It also seems unlikely that Stoker possessed a bag similar to the one the doctor carries, with its instruments and drugs—'the ghastly paraphernalia of our beneficial trade', Van Helsing calls it—although hauling theatrical bags about was very much part of his life.

Such was the care with which Bram Stoker described both the emotions and activities of Dr Van Helsing that he strides from the pages of the book as a fully formed character, so presenting a considerable challenge to any actor who endeavours to play him on either the stage or screen. The man who first did so, Edward Van Sloan, sensed this from the very beginning.

'I have to confess that I had not read the book before I was approached to appear in the New York stage production of Dracula,' he recalled nearly forty years later, when the vampire Count was firmly established as a worldwide cult figure. 'But I did so straight away, and found Van Helsing to be a fascinating and complex man—a man with as open a mind to superstition as he had to science. Nothing seemed too outlandish for him, and he never treated even the wildest of his patients' stories with anything other than courtesy and the closest attention. I don't think I had ever had such a demanding part before.'

Edward Van Sloan was of Dutch extraction—his real name being Van Sloun—and he was born in San Francisco on November 1, 1882. He was educated at the University of California at Berkeley and while there began to develop his interest and talent as an actor by appearing in weekly plays staged by the Professor of German Dramatic Literature—all spoken in German.

Because of the precarious nature of acting, Van Sloan was encouraged by his parents to become a commercial artist, but when he grew tired of this he joined a local repertory company and made his debut in *Under the Greenwood Tree*. In time this led to bigger rôles and finally appearances on Broadway.

'I was usually cast in romantic plays and I actually preferred comedies,' he recalled. 'So it was a bit of a surprise when I was offered a part in *Dracula*. It happened like this. One day the producer Horace Liveright attended a show I was appearing in and suddenly shouted out, "That's *him*! That's the man to play Van Helsing!"'

'Of course I had no idea what he was talking about until we met and he showed me the script for the stage production. But it proved to be a very important moment in my life, for not only did it lead to success on the stage, but later got me into films where I played Van Helsing in two pictures and then did a number of other supernatural parts.'

The play *Dracula* opened at the Fulton Theatre in New York in October 1927, Van Sloan co-starring with Bela Lugosi. Playing Van Helsing week in and week out soon made him very familiar with the rôle, and it was not altogether a surprise to him when Universal Pictures decided to film the story in 1931 and

Edward Van Sloan as
Van Helsing and Bela
Lugosi as Dracula in a
publicity shot for the
1931 movie.

Professor Van Helsing
at work in *Dracula*
(1931) with co-stars
David Manners and
Helen Chandler.

asked him to recreate the rôle for the cinema. Nor that his stage co-star—and now friend—Bela Lugosi, should be Dracula.

'But when I first saw myself on film I wanted to scream and run away, I thought I was so awful,' said Edward. 'I said to myself, "Is that all you've learnt about acting after appearing in 150 or so plays?" I just couldn't believe that Dracula would be a success in the cinema and I felt I should have stayed on the stage!'

Dracula was, as we know, a runaway success and Edward's portrayal of Van Helsing was praised by several of the critics for the dignity, authority and, above all, reality he brought to his character in what was, after all, a fantasy story.

'They actually made me up to look much older than I was,' Edward recalled, 'but with my Dutch ancestry I did not have too much trouble duplicating Dr Van Helsing's manner of speech. In fact, there weren't a great many differences between the stage version and the film, though I do recall one. On the stage, in the famous scene where Van Helsing confronts Dracula with a betraying mirror, we used a full-length wall mirror, and as soon as he saw it he tossed a vase as it and shattered it. In the film this became a small mirror box and I don't believe the scene was anywhere near as dramatic.

'One thing I *did* enjoy doing for the film was the epilogue, when I had to come from behind the curtain to warn the audience that vampires do exist. I had done this so many times on the stage it really was second nature to me. I'm sorry to hear, though, that it has been cut from many of the prints of the film and is not very often seen.'

Edward enjoyed working with Bela Lugosi who, he said, was a 'kind, rather insecure man who let his fame spoil his life'.

'My dear wife never allowed me to get swollen-headed, even when I started getting fan mail from all over the place,' he said. 'Do you know, a lot of these letters were addressed to "Dr Van Helsing" and some even asked me to help them get rid of vampires that the writers said were after their blood! Why, there was even one letter from Transylvania!'

Although Edward Van Sloan was destined to appear in only one more film as Dr Van Helsing—*Dracula's Daughter*, made in 1936, in which the Count himself did not appear—he was to be known for this rôle for the rest of his life. Perhaps the enthusiastic reviews were in part responsible, *Variety* of May 2, 1936, speaking for many people when it said, 'Edward Van Sloan who played the scientist in the original film is here again and just as convincing.'

But Edward still found it strange that two pictures should overshadow the whole of his career. 'Despite all the other horror pictures I made, like *Frankenstein* and *The Mummy* with Boris Karloff and *The Phantom Creeps*, one of several more I did with Bela Lugosi, I was always Dr Van Helsing to critics and audiences alike! I couldn't escape him even when I retired—people would still stop by my house and point it out as the place where "the man who killed Dracula lived!"'

Edward Van Sloan died in his San Francisco home on March 6, 1964, one of the pioneers of the horror film cult which has persisted to this day. His last words might well have been uttered by Van Helsing himself: 'Always take your work seriously, always take your trade seriously, but never, never take *yourself* seriously.'

*   *   *

Peter Cushing, who has become best known as the archetypal modern Dr Van Helsing, is just as modest and self-effacing a man as his American predecessor. And he, too, has been praised by critics and fans for the 'dedicated and dignified' way in which he portrayed the doctor in some five films between 1958 and 1974.

In Peter's case, I have had the pleasure of knowing him for some years and also co-authored a book with him, *Tales of a Monster Hunter*, in 1977. I know how seriously he has always approached the part and how well he has come to understand the character of the 'Vampire Hunter'.

'To me, Van Helsing is the essence of good pitted against the essence of evil,' he once explained. 'I believe that the Dracula films have the same appeal as the old morality plays, with the struggle of good over evil, and good always triumphing in the end.'

Peter was born in Kenley, Surrey, on May 26, 1913, and, after an unhappy period as a surveyor's clerk, went into repertory theatre. Failing to make any

Professor Van Helsing uses both ancient superstition and modern medicine in his battles against vampires—garlic on the one hand, and blood transfusions on the other: (*left*) in *Brides of Dracula* (1960) and (*below*) *The Horror of Dracula* (1958).

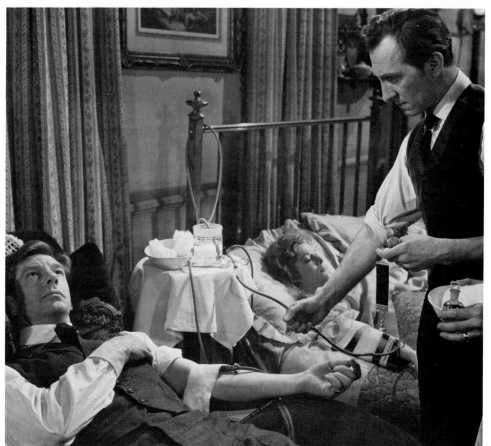

(*Opposite*) The best known exponent of the rôle of Professor Van Helsing—Peter Cushing in a 1960 publicity still.

headway, he took a bold gamble and bought a ticket to Hollywood in search of film rôles. Though he did not achieve stardom, he appeared in movies with several famous names, including Louis Hayward and Laurel and Hardy, and returned to Britain better equipped as an actor; as a result he was soon busy in television and later in films.

It was as Baron Frankenstein in Hammer Films' *The Curse of Frankenstein* (1957) that he made his breakthrough; then, the following year, as Van Helsing in *The Horror of Dracula* with Christopher Lee, he became famous. He had read the Bram Stoker novel as a teenager and had also seen Edward Van Sloan's performances in the two earlier pictures.

'I was immediately attracted to the rôle when it was offered to me,' he says today. 'I suppose in a way it is possible that I was pre-ordained to play Van Helsing. For although I am not a religious man, I do try to live by Christian ethics and I believe in the truth as set forth in the New Testament. I can see so many of the elements of good and evil in life, and this seemed to give me added strength in my screen battles with the powers of darkness.'

While filming *The Horror of Dracula*, he was quoted on his opinion of Van Helsing: 'He is such an intriguing man, dedicated and determined, not to say brave in the face of great danger. I have put a lot of time into my research for the rôle and find myself admiring the man more the better I get to know him.'

And indeed he did get to know him a great deal better after the success of that picture and the critical admiration of his performance. *Variety*, for instance, in its issue of May 7, 1958, said, 'Peter Cushing is impressive as the painstaking scientist-doctor who solves the mystery.'

In the next decade he appeared as Van Helsing in *Brides of Dracula* (1960), *Dracula AD 1972* (in which he played both Van Helsing and his modern day descendant), *The Satanic Rites of Dracula* (1973) and *The Legend of the Seven Golden Vampires* (1974) in which, for the first time, he was without Christopher Lee as an adversary.

Interviewed at this time, he said prophetically, 'The problem with the Dracula series is finding new kinds of variations. Because, like the Western, where the audience expects the gun-fight in the saloon or main street, you must have a man who lives on human blood. The writers have tried many ideas, including bringing the central characters into the modern era, but they are wearing a bit thin.'

Peter also had every sympathy with his friend Christopher Lee's desire not to go on with the series.

'He just doesn't want to keep on playing in the sort of Dracula films he has been playing—"Dracula in the Dark", "Dracula Meets Frankenstein", "Search the House for Dracula" and that sort of thing. As he once said to me, the Van Helsing character, even though it's the same character, is more interesting; but all he has to do as Dracula is stand in a corner, show his fangs, and hiss. I do see his point, but I'm sure if a good one was to come along he would do it.'

Peter still speaks of Christopher Lee with great affection. 'We were actually

Van Helsing (Peter
Cushing) saves himself
from becoming a
vampire after being
bitten in *Brides of
Dracula*, by undergoing
an ordeal by fire.

introduced on the set of *The Curse of Frankenstein* in 1956 and I always say that I met him first in his creature make-up and when he took it off I screamed! He's been such a dear friend. And it's taken tremendous courage on his part to break away from horror films and succeed in something different. It takes great courage in this business to turn away from something that's sure and try something that isn't. But I think he will play Dracula again if and when a definitive version is done.'

Peter, for his part, has no reservations about playing Van Helsing again should the opportunity arise, though, now that he is in his seventies, he feels he might be a little too old and frail for the part.

'Somehow, though, the doctor is an ageless figure in the same way that Baron Frankenstein and Sherlock Holmes are. I am sure he is destined for many more battles with Dracula because the public interest in them is as strong as ever. Wherever Bram Stoker is, I bet he must be looking on with amazement at what has happened to his story over the years!'

Stoker might also be surprised that Peter Cushing can claim to be the only actor to have played both Van Helsing *and* Dracula. For in 1974 he played Dracula in a French production, *Tendre Dracula*, also known as *Tender Dracula* or *The Confessions of a Bloodsucker*, which was directed by Alain Robbe-Grillet and released in 1977. Initially, the film-makers wanted Christopher Lee as the vampire Count, with Peter as his usual adversary, in what was to be a horror satire showing vampires in a sympathetic light.

'I turned the rôle down,' Christopher Lee later told the press when asked about the film. 'And it was perhaps ironic that Peter Cushing should become Dracula!'

Peter enjoyed the rôle enough to play the Count again that same year in a

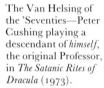

The Van Helsing of the 'Seventies—Peter Cushing playing a descendant of *himself*, the original Professor, in *The Satanic Rites of Dracula* (1973).

cameo rôle in *Madhouse*, a co-production between British and American film-makers, Amicus and American-International.

Recently, not having been seen as Van Helsing on the screen for some years, Peter received a letter from a Dracula fan which he quotes with wry amusement.

'The fellow wrote to me saying, "I've read in a newspaper that you have died. Would you please write and tell me if this is true." I don't know how he expected me to answer if it *was* true, but I wrote back and said, "as far as I know, not yet."'

*   *   *

The latest actor to be cast as the great 'Vampire Hunter' perhaps most graphically illustrates the importance now placed upon the part by film-makers—as a demanding rôle suitable for only the most accomplished of players. The man in question is Lord Olivier, who appeared as the good doctor in the 1979 *Dracula* starring Frank Langella.

As might be expected of perhaps the greatest actor of this century, Olivier brought a style and authority to the rôle which stressed the central importance of Van Helsing in the story.

'I read the book many years ago,' he said during filming in Cornwall in October 1978, 'and I remember being struck by Van Helsing's extraordinary courage. We've all needed some of that working in these stormy conditions!'

The remark might have sounded slightly flippant, but Olivier still brought his usual dedication to the part.

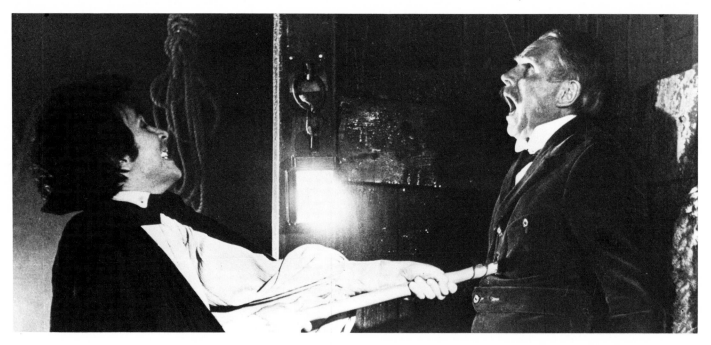

Van Helsing
(Laurence Olivier)
defeated by Dracula
(Frank Langella) in
the 1979 film version of
the novel—but the
battle is still far from
over!

'In fact this is the straightest part I've played in a long time,' he said. 'Frank Langella and Donald Pleasance have the funny lines, but it is up to my character to keep matters under control and on more or less straight lines.'

Olivier, who was born on May 22, 1907, made his acting début in Shakespeare, but it took years of hard work on both stage and screen to be accepted as a major talent. His contribution to the arts was recognised in 1947 when he was knighted, and he was later given a life peerage—the only actor ever to achieve this honour.

Although well into his seventies when he filmed *Dracula*, Lord Olivier threw himself enthusiastically into the rôle of Van Helsing.

'It seemed a little curious filming the sequences from the book, which take place at Whitby in Yorkshire, on the Cornish coast near Tintagel, but I was told the scenery looked more realistic!' he said. 'I know the area has associations with King Arthur who was supposed to have been born in Merlin's Cave near Tintagel, so I suppose that was good for the atmosphere of another story about a mythological character.'

During the filming, Lord Olivier was called upon to do several gruelling scenes while in pursuit of Dracula. 'I do as many of the strictly physical scenes as I can without resorting to the help of a double,' he explained on location. 'I conserve my strength by resting between takes and napping in my dressing-room, so that I can give it everything before the cameras.'

His 'giving it everything' resulted in what is the most memorable performance in the film—better even than that of Frank Langella, in most opinions. Certainly, the failure of the film at the box office could not be attributed in any way to Lord Olivier. His Van Helsing brought a new dimension to the character already developed by Edward Van Sloan and Peter Cushing.

Yet, as all three actors would no doubt be happy to admit, the battle between Dracula and Van Helsing is far from over in the world of the cinema. The two adversaries are now locked together in immortality.

9

'The Bloofer Ladies'

In the half century since the first of the Dracula films were brought to the screen, three strikingly attractive actresses have become inextricably associated with the series—rather like that trio of young ladies in the original novel, who live in the Count's castle and bewitch the unsuspecting Jonathan Harker with their 'brilliant white teeth that shine like pearls against the ruby of their voluptuous lips'. Like the originals, two of these actresses are dark and seductive, while the third is sensual, with 'eyes like pale sapphires'.

The girls are Carol Borland, Barbara Shelley and Barbara Steele—'The Bloofer Ladies' if I might appropriate that evocative expression which Stoker coined to describe the vampire lady who lurks upon Hampstead Heath seeking fresh blood from her victims. Each of these women has made a significant contribution to the Dracula legend in the cinema, and to the horror genre as a whole; for in a genre traditionally dominated by men, they have introduced strong female characters that remain in the memory long after the films have been seen.

Carol Borland was the first female vampire star, appearing with the original Dracula, Bela Lugosi. Barbara Shelley, who co-starred with Christopher Lee, reshaped the entire rôle of women in vampire films. And Barbara Steele has become a cult figure as the vampire lady most men would be willing to risk a stake for. The stories which they all have to tell about their rôles throw interesting new light both on the films and on their illustrious co-stars.

Carol Borland first appeared with the great Bela Lugosi in *Mark of the Vampire* in 1935, and achieved the ultimate ambition of any cinema fan—to appear opposite the star she idolised. In 1931, as a teenager in Los Angeles, she had seen Lugosi in his classic rôle as Dracula, and had been so mesmerised by his performance that she wrote a sequel, *Countess Dracula*, and sent it to him.

Although the copyright restrictions then obtaining prevented the idea being taken any further, Lugosi was impressed enough by the script to begin corresponding with his young admirer. As a direct result of these letters, and some subsequent meetings, Carol was offered a small part in one of Lugosi's stage performances of *Dracula*, and then, in 1935, the part of the Count's daughter, Luna, in *Mark of the Vampire*.

This picture, made by MGM, was not a Dracula film, for Universal had refused to relinquish their hold on the copyright. The scriptwriter, Guy

Endore, and director Tod Browning (who had, of course, directed the original *Dracula*) therefore rechristened the central character Count Mora, and presented him with an undead daughter, Luna. The couple's intentions towards a family occupying what had once been their Castle were, however, very much in the Dracula tradition—as were those of the film-makers, says Carol Borland, reminiscing today about her rôle.

'When we were making *Mark of the Vampire* there was never any question that Lugosi was replaying his famous Dracula part,' she maintains, adding with equal conviction that for her Lugosi has always been *the* Dracula.

'When I say that Dracula is the creation of Lugosi, I do not mean to denigrate the contribution of Bram Stoker. But recall for a moment the description of Count Dracula in the Stoker novel. A seamed, revolting face. A hooked nose. A long, drooping moustache, and small, ember-lit eyes under craggy brows.

'But Dracula as embodied by Lugosi was suave, debonair, fascinating—from the sleek, smooth hair (the sign of the 'Latin Lover' of the period) to the tips of his elegant opera pumps. And that face—so oddly divided. The Satanic widow's peak that pointed to the arrogant arch of the nose, the unexpected blue flame of the eyes, the dark circumflex of brows. And then the radically differing lower part of the face: the curved and pouting mouth above the provocatively oval chin, so deeply cleft.'

Carol believes that this dichotomy best shows up the differences between Lugosi's Dracula and those who have followed him on the screen. 'No one else,' she says, 'has been able to inject that subtle appeal that made his vampire so dreadful—the fact that one was attracted and repelled, loathed and yet was forced to love.

'And isn't this the ultimate horror? Nor the superficial fangs, the claws, the bloodied teeth—but the need to give oneself over to discover what dreadful consummation was achieved behind that merciful, concealing cloak? The modern films, for all their naïve explicitness, can never rival this.'

Director Tod Browning invested as much money and care into the making of *Mark of the Vampire* as he had done with the original *Dracula*. Lavish sets were built, Lugosi's appearance was changed in only the subtlest of ways (his shirt was given a ruff) and scriptwriter Guy Endore employed all his considerable knowledge of the occult for the picture, which was initially to be called *Vampires of Prague*. (Endore, incidentally, had recently written the first great novel of lycanthropy, *The Werewolf of Paris*, published in 1933, and had been especially brought out to Hollywood.)

Carol Borland clearly remembers working with Guy Endore. 'I often spent evenings with him and his wife, and we discussed books, demonology, vampirism—and the Dracula character in particular. In fact, Guy created both in his mind and in the first draft of the script a much more horrifying creature than that which finally appeared on the screen.

'He envisaged a completely new factor for the story. You may remember that in the film, Lugosi's Count appears with a bullet hole in his forehead, which is

(Opposite) Carol Borland, the fan of Bela Lugosi who became his co-star in *Mark of the Vampire* (1935).

112

Bela Lugosi as Count Mora and Carol Borland as his daughter, Luna, in *Mark of the Vampire*.

never fully explained. Well, according to the original script the Count had committed a terrible sin which had lost him his chance of peace after death. He had committed incest with Luna, then strangled her and shot himself.

'This was to give the characters of the two vampires a value of horrid fascination. It could hardly be mentioned, of course, and would have been difficult even to imply on the screen, but Guy was not at all happy when all his suggestions of a bad child, worse father relationship were dropped from the story. Maybe it was this emasculation of the character that made this particular version of the Count less vivid than some of Lugosi's other embodiments.' That, and the contrived finale in which the two vampires are actually revealed to be actors hired to frighten off the inhabitants of the Castle!

Carol has equally vivid memories of her meetings with Bela Lugosi in Hollywood after she had submitted her script for *Countess Dracula*. She was then in her teens, a dark-haired girl with a very striking face and big, luminous eyes. The actor took her to dinner on several occasions, and also window shopping along Hollywood Boulevard.

(*Opposite*) Publicity still for *Mark of the Vampire* with Bela Lugosi and Carol Borland, clearly showing the controversial 'bullet hole' on Lugosi's forehead.

'At the time I never wondered *why* I was chosen as his companion,' she recalls. 'I had a great affection for him as a person and he knew it. He was my idol, yet I was not a "fan". I found him fascinating, intimidating, charming, exasperating, demanding and generous all at the same time. Years later, I began to wonder *what* he had ever seen in me and why it was I had been so fortunate . . .'

Carol pauses for a moment in reflection and then continues. 'I guess it was

812-69

that Lugosi had a natural and open appetite for adulation. He thrived on it. I gave it. He liked young women. I knew him best between my fifteenth and eighteenth years. When we met again in *Mark of the Vampire*, I was twenty-one.

'He was much married and quite a domestic gentleman by then. He was no longer "Bela"—I called him "Mr Lugosi". We chatted together between takes, but I was just the junior member of the cast. Even when we were alone we spoke as colleagues. My "playmate" had gone. We were just a pair of working actors on the same set.'

Although Carol saw Bela Lugosi again in Hollywood on several occasions, she did not actually come into contact with him again until his death. Then she stood by his coffin and mourned the times that had passed. She could not get over the fact that he was wrapped in his Dracula cape.

That moment, and her relationship with Lugosi, helped crystallise her views on the exact nature of Dracula's appeal.

'I agree with the thesis that Count Dracula is a death figure,' she says, choosing her words carefully, 'and that we all have a more or less hidden death wish. To many of us—women particularly—I think he stands for that great unknown factor. He is stronger than other men, more powerful, more feared. What a challenge, what a conquest! Women, who are the guardians and donors of the great life-force, see in him the Dark Enigma whom they can conquer only by being conquered.'

Carol has attempted on several occasions since Lugosi's death to revive interest in her script for *Countess Dracula*. She has also re-enacted her rôle as Luna in a spoof of *My Fair Lady* which she herself wrote as *My Fair Zombie* in 1965.

The film, *Mark of the Vampire*, is regularly re-shown on television, and contains a number of memorable scenes, including one in which she flies across the picture in a 'bat harness'. She recalls that this piece of equipment took two weeks to build, and the cost of the lavish sequence in which it was used, and which took several days' shooting to get right, was over $10,000: a large figure by contemporary standards.

Yet, if this picture was not the huge success of its predecessor, it underlined for Carol Borland what she maintains to this day: 'Many have donned the Count's inky cloak, but for me Dracula is Bela Lugosi and Lugosi is Dracula.'

* * *

Barbara Shelley, the second of the 'Bloofer Ladies', shares a conviction equally as strong as Carol Borland's that the actor *she* played opposite was *the* Count Dracula. In her case it was Christopher Lee, the star of the hugely successful series of Dracula pictures made by Hammer Films in England from the late 'fifties to early 'seventies.

'Christopher had a mesmeric presence on the screen,' she says. 'That brooding face, the strong jaw-line and dark eyes hinted at sexuality and menace without him even having to open his mouth and show his fangs. He was certainly my idea of Count Dracula, particularly in the earlier films, though I

(*Opposite*) The lovely vampire lady, Barbara Shelley.

think his disenchantment with the rôle shows in some of the later ones.'

Barbara, an auburn-haired beauty with bewitching brown eyes, has been described as the best actress to have appeared in the Hammer horror films, and certainly the best of its female vampires. The show business 'bible', *Variety*, for instance, in reviewing her picture *Dracula—Prince of Darkness* in January 1966, said: 'Barbara Shelley, a beautiful and much underrated actress, who appears to be trapped in the horror business, makes a spirited vampire.'

Barbara's performance was as skilfully crafted as Christopher Lee's own, and in hindsight it can be seen that just as this film established Lee as *the* Dracula, so it put her at the forefront of the leading vampire ladies.

Before entering the film business, Barbara was a model and was once described as 'the face that launched new fashions galore and appeared on the front of most of the world's top glossy magazines'. Born in London in 1936, she overcame what she describes as a terrible shyness and uncontrollable blushing through working as a model and then spending three years making some 15 films in the production-line studios of Italy.

'I became a real Italian spitfire,' she recalls, 'but none of the pictures amounted to much, and it wasn't until I returned to England and got an important part in Hammer Films' production of *Camp on Blood Island* in 1958 that my career started to take off.

'And from one bloody film I went to another, if you'll excuse the pun,' she says with one of her typically audacious smiles. This second 'bloody' picture was to give her her first experience of the vampire legend when she was cast opposite the famous Shakespearian actor, Sir Donald Wolfit, in *Blood of the Vampire*, made by Eros Films in 1958.

'It wasn't a Dracula picture,' she recalls, 'although the story was set in Transylvania in the 1880s, about the same time Dracula was around. Sir Donald Wolfit was Dr Callistratus, a vampire who had got himself the job of doctor at a prison for the criminally insane. I played Madeleine, the fiancée of one of the prisoners who, as you might expect, had been wrongly imprisoned. So I became the Doctor's housekeeper to find out why he was carrying out blood tests on the prisoners and also to try to get my fiancé released.

'Of course, the Doctor discovers who I really am and I only escape being drained of blood at the very last moment. It did give me a taste of things to come, though!' In the next few years she played several more fantasy rôles including *Village of the Damned* (1960) and *The Gorgon* (1964).

Barbara was even more beautiful and statuesque when she was cast in *Dracula—Prince of Darkness* which was filmed in 1965.

'I didn't take a lot of persuading,' she recalls, 'because I loved working at Bray Studios which had such a stimulating atmosphere. I also really enjoyed working with Christopher Lee because he is such a good companion and has a very rich sense of humour.'

In *Dracula—Prince of Darkness*, Barbara played Helen, a prim if somewhat unhappy Victorian wife, who is touring the Carpathian mountains with her husband. Ignoring warnings not to visit Castle Dracula, Helen is seized and

(*Opposite*) Brabara Shelley in her first vampire film with Sir Donald Wolfit, *Blood of the Vampire* (1958).

118

A tasty morsel for
Dracula—Barbara
Shelley with
Christopher Lee in a
publicity shot for
*Dracula, Prince of
Darkness* (1965).

bitten in the throat by the revived vampire Count and becomes a most
seductive vampiress herself.

Talking about the rôle during filming she said, 'Helen is the epitome of evil, a
frightened lady who becomes the victim of vicious sexuality . . . So you can see
I'm not particularly obsessed with preserving a public image, or being a starry
girl.'

Later, she explained her motivation more fully. 'I attacked the part of the
vampire by, as usual, looking for a peg to hang my hat on—or should I say
fangs? I found in it a likeness to the Greek Furies and played it as the epitome of
all evil.

'As to the eroticism of the legend, so much has already been said and written
on that subject by people far more capable than I that I can add very little.
Perhaps the eroticism is heightened by the night symbols, and by the unbridled
greed and determination of the vampire to achieve its ends. There is always
something fascinating and repellent about a completely uncontrolled and rabid
emotion.'

Barbara's rich, deep voice, which has been described by her friends as

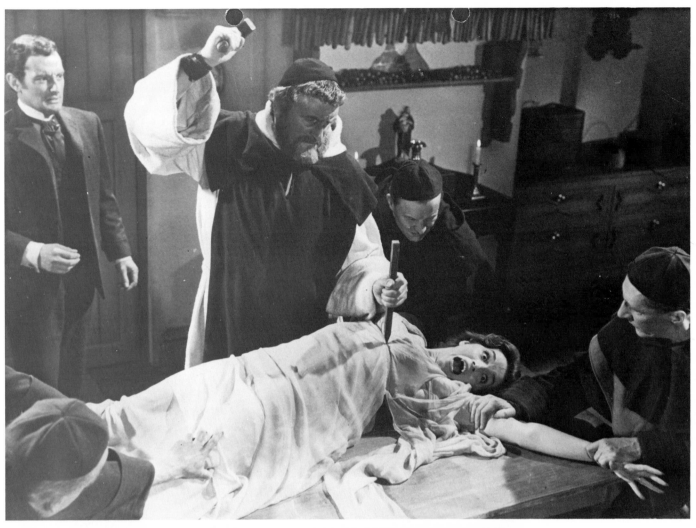

The fate of the vampire—Barbara Shelley being staked to a table by Father Sandor (Andrew Keir) in *Dracula, Prince of Darkness*. This was the first time such a gruesome sequence had ever been shown on the screen.

'smouldering mink' and which she says makes her the world's only woman bass-baritone—was used to great effect in the film. 'When I screamed in Dracula—and I screamed a great deal—I sounded like a sea-lion!' she says with a smile.

A sensational moment in the picture was the gruesome sequence in which Barbara's reign of terror as a vampire was finally put to an end when she was staked to a table by a group of monks. This was the first time such a scene had been shown in such graphic detail in a vampire film.

Alexander Walker of the London *Evening Standard* made a particular reference to this in his review of January 6, 1966. 'One bite,' he wrote, 'and staid tourist Barbara Shelley is Dracula's hunting mate—and wonders it does for her appearance till she gets a stake driven through her. Connoisseurs of these things will note the lethal spot is higher up the bosom and more central than the heart!'

Barbara very nearly made a return to the screen in another Dracula film in 1972. Word leaked into the press that Hammer Films were planning to make *Dracula Walks the Night* which would be the most ambitious picture in the series to date. Christopher Lee and Peter Cushing were to play their traditional rôles, with Barbara as another beauty drawn into Dracula's service.

The script was planned to trace the 'origins' of Dracula back to Vlad the Impaler and then move forward to London in the year 1895, with Van Helsing joining forces with the great Sherlock Holmes to fight Dracula now loose on the streets of the capital! This ingenious idea had come from scriptwriters Jimmy Sangster and Richard Matheson, and the leading Hammer director, Terrence Fisher, was to direct.

Another intriguing piece of proposed casting was that of Jack Palance, to play Dracula's servant, Macata. As we know, when Palance *did* go before the cameras it was as the vampire Count himself, in the 1973 film. Sadly, this costly project never materialised and enthusiasts were denied what might well have been the best of all Hammer's Dracula pictures.

Barbara Shelley herself has now turned her back on the horror genre, but her impact on the legend is beyond question and many an actress who has since attempted to bring some verisimilitude to the part of a female vampire has owed much to her bench-mark performance. As the American magazine, *Little Shop of Horrors*, said in April 1978, 'She was a classy lady—bringing a touch to her rôles that none of the latter-day Hammer hormone cases could ever hope to achieve. She is sorely missed in these days of overdeveloped but undertrained "actresses".'

*   *   *

The third of our ladies, Barbara Steele, had a similarly stunning impact on the vampire screen legend with her very first picture in the genre. She, too, is sorely missed in the cinema today, although her cult-status remains unchanged.

Raven-haired and green-eyed, Barbara is still referred to as 'The Queen of

Barbara Steele—the
world's favourite
vampiress—sometimes
known as 'Miss
Dracula'.

Terror' and 'Alias: Miss Dracula'. The American Count Dracula Society gave her its premier award for contributions to the genre in 1973, and *Telerama*, the French journal, only recently called her 'la Marilyn des disciples du Comte Dracula'.

Although she has, in fact, made a variety of films, it is for the horror pictures that she is best known—and in particular three vampire films. The first of these, *Revenge of the Vampire* (also known as *Black Sunday* and *The Hour When Dracula Comes*) made her an overnight star when it was shown in Italy in 1960. Directed by Mario Bava, a cameraman-turned-director who was destined to earn a considerable reputation as a result of his horror pictures, it told the story of Princess Asa, a two-hundred-year-old vampiress revived by a drop of blood to wreak terrible vengeance on the descendants of those who had originally buried her alive in a tomb.

The reviews which greeted the picture were ecstatic. In America, Drake Douglas called the film 'the most original vampire tale since Bela Lugosi's *Dracula*', and went on: 'The slow revival of the vampire woman with the dripping of the blood, the crawling of the spiders and centipedes, the resurrection from the grave of her satanic assistant . . . are superb instances of the tremendous effects visual horror may have on an audience.'

In Britain opinions were just as keen—although the censor promptly refused

123

the picture a certificate and it was some seven years before it was publicly viewed in this country. Nonetheless, R. Michael Johnson enthused, 'Miss Steele, an unknown (until recently) actress, gives one of the most chilling portrayals of a vampire seen on the screen, ranking in my opinion with Christopher Lee's new interpretation of Count Dracula.'

For Barbara Steele, born in December 1938 on a boat travelling between Ireland and England, and trained as a painter before taking up a career in acting, the reception was quite a surprise. She had tried to break into films both in Britain (where she was the last female to be signed by the J. Arthur Rank Organisation for its 'charm school') and in Hollywood (where 20th Century Fox kept her 'sitting on a beach waiting to be called for two years'). So, in desperation, she went to Italy.

'Right out of the blue I was offered *Revenge of the Vampire*,' she recalls. 'I think the original title was *Mask of the Demon*, but these things change names all over the world. Anyhow, I did it in a panic. After not working for two years, you take any film.'

It was perhaps fated that Barbara *should* succeed in horror films, for she explains that one of her very first rôles as a young repertory actress was a witch in John Van Druten's play *Bell, Book and Candle*, at the Citizen's Theatre in Glasgow. It was here, too, that she was spotted by a Rank talent scout who proceeded to put her pretty foot on the first rung of the ladder to stardom.

The critical and box-office success of *Revenge of the Vampire* resulted in similar scripts being offered to Barbara, and among the pictures she made in the next few busy years were *The Pit and the Pendulum*, based on the famous Edgar Allan Poe story, for Roger Corman in America (1961), *The Terror of Dr Hitchcock* (1962) and *The Spectre* (1962), both in Italy.

In 1964 she made her second venture into the vampire theme in a joint Italian/French co-production, *Castle of Blood* (also known as *Danse Macabre*), directed by Antonio Margheriti. In this, she played one of a family of vampires who terrify to death a man foolish enough to spend a night in a haunted house.

Barbara has an amusing and rather erotic memory of making this picture. 'My co-star, Margaret Robsham, and I had to mime a lesbian love scene,' she says. 'But she just freaked out at the prospect of kissing me. The director, Antonio Margheriti, got very angry with her and finally tried telling her, "Imagine you are kissing Ugo (her husband, Ugo Tognazzi) not Barbara!" We got it right in the end, but I've never found out if the scene was used in the finished picture.'

The following year, 1965, Barbara made *Revenge of the Blood Beast* in which she appeared for the second time as a two-hundred-year-old vampire, this time returning to a Communist-occupied Transylvania. There was no Dracula in the picture, however, but instead a Dr 'Von' Helsing who boasts about how he killed the vampire Count—and then dispatched his female compatriot in the same manner.

This was the last of Barbara's trio of vampire movies. But their impact generated a cult following in Europe which pursues her to this day—not

entirely to her pleasure. She does, however, have happy memories of making her horror pictures.

Barbara Steele in the film that made her famous, *Revenge of the Vampire* (1960).

'We had a marvellous time,' she recalls. 'The only thing I resent—because it is a bloody difficult genre—is that these films can stop you from doing others because of the terrible image bag they get you into.

'They were all made very quickly, too. We'd work with three cameras for 16 hours a day. It was a good job they were horror films—a girl can't do close-ups after 16 hours!

'Seriously,' she goes on, 'any script—any circumstance—that is not believable, is much more difficult to do, to make something happen, than a more realistic drama.

'I got superstitious about the films, too. I may not believe in fate, but those pictures were a bit chancy, a little spooky. I swear I'm never going to climb out of another bloody coffin as long as I live!'

Of her films, Barbara rates *Castle of Blood* among her favourites—despite the fact it also has the reputation of showing her in the nude!

'It wasn't *me*,' she affirms. 'I've never done a nude film yet. But the people who made the pictures were always doing inserts—tricky little things like sticking in somebody with your wig on and completely nude. You know, four feet tall with size 48 bosoms and she comes on pretending to be me.'

125

A dramatic moment from the vampire picture, *Castle of Blood* (1964), one of Barbara Steele's favourite movies.

Barbara Steele can, however, claim the unique distinction of having appeared opposite the three greatest stars of modern horror films, Boris Karloff, Vincent Price and Christopher Lee.

'They are all such suave gentlemen—for bloodsuckers,' she jokes. 'But then so were Count Dracula and Baron Frankenstein. They had such fantastic ancestral histories. We're just peasants in relation to them.'

Barbara has a special affection for Christopher Lee, and if anyone could lure her back to the screen where she has not appeared since 1979, in *Piranha*, it is probably he.

'Christopher has often called me up and said, "I've had enough of seeing the producers get all the money—why don't we produce a film ourselves?" Then we've had a drunken lunch and laid plans to make a really gorgeous horror movie, with lots of sincerity and not another of those cheap, write-as-we-shoot efforts. You know, there really *hasn't* been a classic since the 'thirties.'

Barbara is not completely lost to the world of films, for she was recently associate producer on the $35 million mini-TV series, *Winds of War*, starring Robert Mitchum. But to her fans she remains the only actress in the world to have starred, survived and excelled in the male-dominated field of horror films, and arguably the most delectable actress ever to have put on vampire fangs and sucked the blood of a willing victim—the 'Bloofer Lady' *par excellence*!

126

10

The *Wurdalak* Who Might Have Been Dracula

One of the last, most tantalising questions about the Dracula legend is this: could Boris Karloff, the most famous of all horror film stars, have played the first Dracula and so changed the whole image of the Count on the screen? His name was on the long list of those considered by Universal Pictures for the part in 1931, and although the rôle went to Bela Lugosi and Karloff only played a vampire once on the screen, his name remains linked with the legend.

Unlike Bela Lugosi, who was an established stage actor in 1931, Karloff was still trying to make an impact in films, although he had already got several dozen character parts behind him following his Hollywood début in 1919 as a Mexican bandit in *His Majesty, the American* for United Artists. The fact that he had appeared in most of these films as a foreigner—anything from an Arab to a French-Canadian, and almost invariably a villain—got him on the Universal list for Dracula when it was decided the part had to be played by a non-American. The fact that he was actually an English gentleman by birth also weighed in his favour to play the impeccably-mannered Count from Transylvania.

Bela Lugosi got the part for all the right reasons: his looks, his style of acting, the fact he had been born in Transylvania—and, perhaps most importantly of all, because he was intimately familiar with the rôle after playing it on the stage for two years.

However, Karloff's big break was to come almost immediately after this when Universal decided to follow *Dracula* with that other horror classic, *Frankenstein.* The part of the creature was first offered to Lugosi by the director James Whale, but he turned it down flat. He was not prepared to play a non-speaking rôle almost submerged in make-up. Karloff, on the other hand, grabbed at the chance—and the rest is history.

'That part was what we call a "natural",' Karloff was to say years later. 'Any actor who played it was destined for success.'

The road to success had been a long one for the actor born William Henry Pratt, the son of a civil servant in the British foreign service, on November 23, 1887, in Camberwell, South London. William was the youngest of eight sons

127

Boris Karloff as
Dracula—an
imaginative
interpretation by
American artist, Ed
Kosterville.

and one daughter, and almost immediately the family moved to Chase Green
Avenue in Enfield, Middlesex, were he grew up.

I have always been interested in Karloff's early years because Enfield
happens to be my birthplace, too. And I remember, years ago, one of his
relatives who was still living in the area telling me that young William had
started to develop an interest in the theatre when he was very young, as a result
of one of his older brothers, George, going on the stage and scoring a success
that was a source of pride to the whole family.

In fact, William's first stage appearance took place when he was just nine
years old, playing the Demon King in a production of *Cinderella* at the local
church hall. It was a singularly appropriate début for him considering what lay
ahead—and the significance was not lost on him when he talked about his
career much later.

'It was a curious thing,' he remarked, 'but I sort of tasted blood as the Demon

Boris Karloff in the
early 'Thirties, when
Universal filmed the
first *Dracula*.

King in my first stage part and I knew right then and there that that was what I wanted to do for the rest of my life. And if you want something *that* badly, there's only one thing to do—go out and get it!'

Which is precisely what young William did, after completing his education. In 1909 he emigrated to Canada, and after a brief period as a lumberjack, joined a touring theatre company and for a decade played supporting rôles all over Canada and the USA. It was at this time that he decided his real name, Pratt, was hardly a suitable one for an actor, and so he adopted Karloff after an ancestor of his mother and Boris because he just happened to like it!

In 1919, tiring of the constant touring, he decided to try his luck in the silent movies in Hollywood. There followed ten years of intermittent work, subsidised by truck driving, before sound arrived. Then his commanding screen presence and fine stage-trained voice at last provided him with the necessary assets to become a star. Those assets, plus the part in *Frankenstein* which catapulted him to fame, in the following years made him one of the biggest names in the horror genre.

Although Boris Karloff did not play Dracula in 1931, he was starred a year later in a film which some experts have seen as a remake of the vampire story in a different setting. This was *The Mummy*, and I quote from Donald F. Glut's excellent study, *The Dracula Book* (1975):

> To an extent, *The Mummy*, directed by Karl Freund and starring Boris Karloff in the title rôle, was a 'remake' of Dracula. [Freund, incidentally, was the cameraman on *Dracula*.] Karloff portrayed Im-ho-tep, an Egyptian buried alive and revived in the twentieth century. Masquerading as Ardoth Bey, the living mummy seeks to reclaim his reincarnated lover. Edward Van Sloan played an archaeologist with a Van Helsing-type knowledge of the supernatural and a fervent desire to destroy Ardoth Bey before he can transform the reincarnated princess into a creature like himself. The battle of wits between Ardoth Bey and his opponent are similar to those between Count Dracula and Van Helsing.

It was not until 1934 that Boris Karloff actually appeared with the other 'King of Horror', Bela Lugosi, in *The Black Cat*. Naturally, the two men shared equal billing in this story of devil worship in which Karloff was the head of a satanic cult and Lugosi his avowed opponent.

Making the picture provided the two men with a chance to get to know each other and a rare photograph included in this book shows them together on the set. In 1967, in an interview in his comfortable, book-lined flat in Cadogan Square, London, where he settled for the closing years of his life, Karloff talked about Lugosi.

'Although we worked on several films together, we didn't socialise,' he said. 'You see, our lives, our tastes were quite different. Ours was simply a professional relationship. But I have warm recollections of him. I have only seen a few of his films, but I do recall seeing him play Dracula—not on film, but the stage.

(*Opposite*) Hollywood's two greatest horror film stars, Karloff and Lugosi, pictured in 1934.

131

'Bela was a fine actor and a great technician—he was worth a lot more than he got. Poor man, he had a very tragic life, you know. A very sad life. He was a charming person, but in some ways a fool to himself.

'He never took the trouble to master the English language to the degree he should have done. When he got to America he surrounded himself with his Hungarian friends and was quite content to do so. I mean, look at Peter Lorre. He was Hungarian, yet he mastered English almost to perfection. But Bela was a kind and lovable man and I remember our work together with affection.'

He also recalled an amusing publicity stunt set up in October 1932 to help promote *The Black Cat*, in which the two 'Kings of Horror' were supposedly trying to scare each other to death with frightening stories about their work. Karloff naturally talked about his rôle as the Frankenstein creature, and then Lugosi retaliated as Dracula. A report of this 'challenge' between the two screen monsters records Bela Lugosi's words.

'Boris,' he said, 'women are thrilled by Dracula, the suave one. Women love the horrible, the creepy, more than men. Why does a woman always tell the story of her husband's death so often and with such relish? Why does she go to cemeteries? Tenderness? Grief? Bah! It's because she likes to be hurt, tortured, terrified!

'Ah, Boris, to win a woman, take her with you to see *Dracula*, the movie. As she sees me, the bat-like vampire, swoop through an open casement into some girl's boudoir, there to sink teeth into neck and drink blood, she will thrill through every nerve and fibre. That is your cue to draw close to her, Boris. When she is limp as a rag, take her where you will, do with her what you will. And, especially, Boris, bite her on the neck.

'The love bite, it is the beginning!' Lugosi went on. 'In the end, you, too, Boris, will become a vampire. You will live five hundred years. You will sleep in mouldy graves at night, and make fiendish love to beauties by day. You will see generations live and die. You will see a girl baby born to some woman, and wait a mere sixteen to eighteen years for her to grow up, so that you can sink fangs into a soft white neck and drink a scarlet stream. You will be irresistible, for you will have in your powerful body the very heat of hell, the virility of Satan. And some day, of course, you will be discovered—a knife will be plunged into you and you will plummet like a stone into the bottomless, sulphurous pit.Yes, Boris, that's the end—for you! For us! For, look at *me*, Boris . . .'

According to Boris Karloff's recollection, the contest ended in an honourable draw—although it did generate some splendid headlines in the newspapers and film magazines.

Karloff also appeared with Lugosi in six other pictures: *The Raven* (1935), based on two Edgar Allan Poe stories; *The Invisible Ray* (1936), directed by Lambert Hillyer; *Son of Frankenstein* (1939), in which Lugosi gave perhaps his best performance, apart from Dracula, as a hunch-back shepherd named Igor; *Black Friday* (1940), a gangster picture; *You'll Find Out* (1941), a mystery which also starred Peter Lorre; and *The Body Snatchers* (1945), based on the famous Robert Louis Stevenson story.

Boris Karloff as Dr
Gustav Niemann who
reanimates the
skeleton of Dracula
into a living being in
House of Frankenstein
(1944).

It was not, however, in association with Bela Lugosi that Karloff made his contribution to the vampire legend.

There is a persistent story in Hollywood that when Universal Pictures were preparing their sequel to *Dracula*, called *Dracula's Daughter*, and eventually made in 1936 by Lambert Hillyer, they originally planned to star Boris Karloff instead of Bela Lugosi as the Count, who would only make a fleeting appearance in the picture.

Whether this was because Lugosi simply did not want to play the rôle then, or because of his commitments elsewhere, has never been satisfactorily explained. As it was, the central rôle was taken by the London-born actress Gloria Holden as Countess Marya Zaleska, Dracula's ill-fated daughter, waited on hand and foot by a sinister-looking servant named Sandor, played by Irving Pichel (later to become a film director). Sandor appears far more like a vampire than his mistress, and it is my belief that it was *this* rôle that was ear-marked for Boris Karloff.

In the event, no Count Dracula appeared in the picture, save for a wax dummy in the likeness of Bela Lugosi which was seen in a few scenes. One important actor from the earlier picture who did reappear was Edward Van Sloan playing Dr Van Helsing once again.

Not until 1944 did Karloff actually appear in his first vampire picture, *House of Frankenstein*, in which he played Dr Gustav Niemann, a mad scientist who discovers the skeleton of Count Dracula in a Chamber of Horrors show and revives him. The Count was played by Lugosi's successor, John Carradine.

In one memorable scene, Karloff confronted an audience in the Chamber of Horrors and, opening a coffin to reveal a skeleton with a stake between its ribs, declaimed: 'Dare I but remove this stake from where his heart once beat and he would rise from the grave! Ladies and gentlemen—the actual skeleton of Count Dracula, the vampire!'

In the sequel to this film made the following year, *House of Dracula*, which also starred John Carradine, Karloff was seen for a few moments in a clip taken from his earlier picture, *The Bride of Frankenstein* (1935).

That same year Karloff tangled with a very different kind of vampire—a beautiful girl who is plaguing a small burial island off the coast of Greece—in *The Isle of the Dead* directed by Mark Robson and produced by Val Lewton. He played a Greek general who discovers that one of the tombs is empty and others had been violated. Although the film is eerie and at times quite gruesome, it is something of a mystery why it should have been banned from being shown in Britain for ten years.

The year 1965 finally saw Boris Karloff play a vampire and, by so doing, complete the roster of monster parts he had taken since his début in *Frankenstein*. This film was *Black Sabbath*, based on a classic Russian vampire short story, 'The Wurdalak' by Alexey Tolstoy.

Boris had to travel to Italy to film this story of a poor Siberian peasant, Gorca, whose family are being terrorised by a vampire known as a *wurdalak*. After a dogged pursuit he finally corners the creature and beheads it, taking the

(*Opposite*) Karloff the Wurdalak—a still from his memorable performance as a Russian vampire in *Black Sabbath* (1965).

134

head back home with him in a sack. But by the time he has returned to his family, Gorca himself has become a *wurdalak* and is compelled to turn all of them into blood drinkers like himself.

Under the direction of Mario Bava, who had previously made several other fine vampire pictures, including *Revenge of the Vampire* with Barbara Steele in 1960, Boris turned in a beautifully restrained performance that was both chilling and engrossing to watch. With this one appearance he added a whole new dimension to the vampire on the screen, and it is no wonder that *Black Sabbath* now has the reputation of being a horror classic.

Karloff not only narrated this story but also did his own English dubbing, and he was naturally proud of the film's excellent reception at the hands of both critics and audiences. He was only too aware of the difficulties being faced by the cinema industry in finding new types of vampire stories, and indeed said so in an interview given later that year.

'I haven't seen any of the new Dracula or Frankenstein films,' he said, 'but I imagine the scriptwriters must have a real problem trying to find something new to put in them. Though I'm sure they're made quite well, there is a modern tendency with the so-called horror film to introduce shocks just for their own sake. This I believe to be wrong. Shocks should evolve naturally from the situations and stories. They should *not* be forced into a film without excuse.'

He also elaborated on his own career. 'I have really enjoyed playing grotesque characters; they fascinate me and have brought me stardom and a handsome income. I protest, though, against the labelling of my melodramas as horror pictures. They are bogy stories, that's all. Just bogy stories with the same appeal as thrilling ghost stories or fantastic fairy tales that entertain and enthral in spite of being so much hokum.'

Karloff's 'hokum' is assured of a place in cinema history, and he was widely mourned when he died on February 2, 1969, aged 82. Among the many tributes that were paid to him was one from the Dracula Society who had just awarded him their Ann Radcliffe Award for his contribution to the genre. They were planning to present the award to him at their annual dinner in April, but instead left an empty chair in memory of 'the King of Horror Films who in spirit will always be with us'.

Appendices

I

Transylvanian Superstitions

by Emily de Laszowska Gerard
(1885)

Transylvania might well be termed the land of superstition, for nowhere else does this curious crooked plant of delusion flourish as persistently and in such bewildering variety. It would almost seem as though the whole species of demons, pixies, witches, and hobgoblins, driven from the rest of Europe by the wand of science, had taken refuge within this mountain rampart, well aware that here they would find secure lurking-places, whence they might defy their persecutors yet awhile.

There are many reasons why these fabulous beings should retain an abnormally firm hold on the soil of these parts; and looking at the matter closely we find here no less than three separate sources of superstition.

First, there is what may be called the indigenous superstition of the country, the scenery of which is peculiarly adapted to serve as background to all sorts of supernatural beings and monsters. There are innumerable caverns, whose mysterious depths seem made to harbour whole legions of evil spirits: forest glades fit only for fairy folk on moonlight nights, solitary lakes which instinctively call up visions of water sprites; golden treasures lying hidden in mountain chasms, all of which have gradually insinuated themselves into the minds of the oldest inhabitants, the Rumanians, and influenced their way of thinking, so that these people, by nature imaginative and poetically inclined, have built up for themselves out of the surrounding materials a whole code of fanciful superstition, to which they adhere as closely as to their religion itself.

Secondly, there is here the imported superstition: that is to say, the old German customs and beliefs brought hither seven hundred years ago by the Saxon colonists from their native land, and like many other things, preserved here in greater perfection than in the original country.

Thirdly, there is the wandering superstition of the gypsy tribes, themselves a race of fortune-tellers and witches, whose ambulating caravans cover the country as with a network, and whose less vagrant members fill up the suburbs of towns and villages.

Of course all these various sorts of superstition have twined and intermingled, acted and reacted upon each other, until in many cases it is a difficult matter to determine the exact parentage of some particular belief or custom; but in a general way the three sources I have named may be admitted as a

138

rough sort of classification in dealing with the principal superstitions afloat in Transylvania.

There is on this subject no truer saying than that of Grimm, to the effect that 'superstition in all its manifold varieties constitutes a sort of religion, applicable to the common household necessities of daily life,' and as such, particular forms of superstition may very well serve as guide to the characters and habits of the particular nation in which they are prevalent.

The spirit of evil (or, not to put too fine a point upon it, the devil) plays a conspicuous part in the Rumanian code of superstition, and such designations as the Gregynia Drakuluj (devil's garden), the Gania Drakuluj (devil's mountain), Yadu Drakuluj (devil's hell or abyss), etc. etc., which we frequently find attached to rocks, caverns, or heights, attest the fact that these people believe themselves to be surrounded on all sides by a whole legion of evil spirits.

The devils are furthermore assisted by witches and dragons, and to all of these dangerous beings are ascribed peculiar powers on particular days and at certain places. Many and curious are therefore the means by which the Rumanians endeavour to counteract these baleful influences, and a whole complicated study, about as laborious as the mastering of any unknown language, is required in order to teach an unfortunate peasant to steer clear of the dangers by which he considers himself to be beset on all sides. The bringing up of a common domestic cow is apparently as difficult a task as the rearing of any deer gazelle, and even the well-doing of a simple turnip or potato about as precarious as that of the most tender exotic plant.

Most decidedly evil, however, is the vampire, or *nosferatu*, in whom every Rumanian peasant believes as firmly as he does in heaven or hell. There are two sorts of vampires—living and dead. The living vampire is in general the illegitimate offspring of two illegitimate persons, but even a flawless pedigree will not ensure anyone against the intrusion of a vampire into his family vault, since every person killed by a *nosferatu* becomes likewise a vampire after death, and will continue to suck the blood of other innocent people till the spirit has been exorcised, either by opening the grave of the person suspected and driving a stake through the corpse, or firing a pistol shot into the coffin. In very obstinate cases, it is further recommended to cut off the head and replace it in the coffin with the mouth filled with garlic, or to extract the heart and burn it, strewing the ashes over the grave.

That such remedies are often resorted to, even in our enlightened days, is a well-attested fact, and there are probably few Rumanian villages where such has not taken place within the memory of the inhabitants.

First cousin to the vampire, the long exploded were-wolf of the Germans is here to be found, lingering yet under the name of the *Prikolitsch*. Sometimes it is a dog instead of a wolf, whose form a man has taken either voluntarily or as penance for his sins. In one of the villages a story is still told (and believed) of such a man, who driving home from church on Sunday with his wife, suddenly felt that the time for his transformation had come. He therefore gave over the reins to her, and stepped aside into the bushes, where, murmuring the mystic formula, he turned three somersaults over a ditch. Soon after this the woman, waiting in vain for her husband, was attacked by a furious dog, which rushed, barking, out of the bushes and succeeded in biting her severely, as well as tearing her dress. When, an hour later, this woman reached home alone she was met by her husband, who advanced smiling to meet her, but between his teeth she caught sight of the shreds of her dress which had been bitten out by the dog, and the horror of the discovery caused her to faint away.

Another man used gravely to assert that for more than five years he had gone about in the form of a wolf, leading on a troop of these animals, until a hunter, in striking off his head, restored him to his natural shape.

A French traveller relates an instance of a harmless botanist who, while collecting herbs on a hillside in a crouching attitude, was observed by some peasants at a distance and taken for a wolf. Before they had time to reach him, however, he had risen to his feet and disclosed himself in the form of a man; but this, in the minds of the Rumanians, who now regarded him as an aggravated case of wolf, was but additional motive for attacking him. They were quite sure that he must be a *Prikolitsch*, for only such could change his shape in such an unaccountable manner, and in another minute they were all in full cry after the wretched victim of science, who might have fared badly indeed, had he not happened to gain a carriage on the high road before his pursuers came up.

We do not require to go far for the explanation of the extraordinary tenacity of life of the were-wolf legend in a country like Transylvania, where real wolves still abound. Every winter here brings fresh proof of the boldness and cunning of these terrible animals, whose attacks on flocks and farms are often conducted with a skill which would do honour to a human intellect. Sometimes a whole village is kept in trepidation for weeks together by some particularly audacious leader of a flock of wolves, to whom the peasants not unnaturally attribute a more than animal nature, and one may safely prophesy that so long as the real wolf continues to haunt the Transylvanian forests, so long will his spectre brother survive in the minds of the inhabitants.

II

A Checklist of Vampirism

*From the Thirteenth Century
to the Present Day*

It would be impossible to provide a complete list of all the cases of vampirism—investigated or merely suspected—in a book such as this. Yet I have been able to assemble a short but I believe representative cross-section, beginning (appropriately) in the thirteenth century with one of the earliest authenticated cases and running through to the late twentieth century. There have been innumerable books published on the theme of the vampire in history, and for the reader interested in pursuing this aspect the following works are recommended: *The Vampire in Legend, Fact and Art* by Basil Copper (Hale, 1973); *The Natural History of the Vampire* by Anthony Masters (Hart-Davis, 1972); two books by Montague Summers, *The Vampire: His Kith and Kin* (Kegan Paul, 1928) and *The Vampire in Europe* (Kegan Paul, 1929); and *Vampires and Vampirism* by Dudley Wright (Rider, 1924).

Thirteenth Century
MORAVIA (*c.* 1250)
Several suspected cases of vampirism were reported in this central European country which is now part of Czechoslovakia. At Stadlieb, near Olmutz, a tomb was opened and the body of a presumed vampire was dismembered before being re-buried. Some years later, at another town not far from Olmutz called Liebava, reports circulated that a vampire was leaving its tomb in the local cemetery and attacking sleeping women and children. Those who had seen the vampire said it was a leading citizen of the community who had recently died. A 'vampire hunter' was summoned from neighbouring Hungary and, after hearing the accounts, climbed up the church tower overlooking the cemetery and there kept watch for several nights. When the man saw the vampire emerge from a tomb and disappear into the town, he hurried down and stole the creature's shroud. As soon as the vampire returned and found its shroud missing—says the story—it immediately looked up at the tower which the hunter had reclimbed for safety and began to howl in a most unearthly voice. At this, the man challenged the undead being to come up the tower and retrieve its shroud. The man kept his nerve until the creature had nearly reached him and then knocked it off the building with a spade. Before the vampire could recover from its fall, the 'vampire hunter' descended and cut off its head with the spade.

Fourteenth Century

FRANCE (1310)

Following the Council of Troyes in May, 1310, King Philippe ordered that the corpse of a certain Jehan de Turo be exhumed and destroyed by fire 'on suspicion that he was a vampyre'. Jehan was said to have been foreman of the Tower and an initiate of the Temple who had died a century earlier.

BOHEMIA (1337)

Reports indicate that several vampires manifested themselves at this time from the cloisters of the church at Opatowicze, but the disturbances ceased after the area was exorcised with holy water and a silver cross hung on the wall. Also in Bohemia, at the town of Lewin, a woman called Brodka, who was believed to dabble in sorcery and had died by her own hand, was buried at the local crossroads in 1345. Suicides of evil repute who were not interred in this manner were believed to become vampires after their death.

Fifteenth Century

UPPER STYRIA (1451)

At Gratz in the mountainous regions of Upper Styria, now a Province of Austria, lived Barbara de Cilly, a beautiful woman much loved by Sigismund of Hungary. When close to death, she was apparently saved by the use of a secret ritual devised by Abramerlin the Mage, but as a result was condemned forever after to be a vampire. This woman was the inspiration for *Camilla*, the masterpiece about a female vampire by the Irish writer, Joseph Sheridan Le Fanu.

Sixteenth Century

TURKEY (1523)

A vampire which had been terrorising the people of Sjonica was finally driven away by a courageous man named Ibro who attacked the creature one night with a knife upon which was engraved a lucky symbol to ward off evil spirits. Although the creature fled, never to be seen again, a spot of its blood left behind on the ground proved impossible to remove.

Seventeenth Century

MORAVIA (1617)

A veritable plague of vampires troubled the Moravian town of Egwanschitz for some years, according to contemporary reports. Unfortunately, there is no record as to when or how this terrible situation was resolved.

RUMANIA (1624)

A beautiful and allegedly very beguiling female vampire seduced and then drank the blood of a number of men in the town of Craiova during this year. She was last seen near the River Jiu and, as water is said to be fatal to vampires, is presumed to have drowned.

HUNGARY (1690)

For some years, Arnold Paul, the High Duke of Medreiga, was said to have been regularly attacked by a vampire at Cassova—but then claimed to have put a stop to these attacks by eating earth taken from the dead man's grave and also smearing himself with the creature's blood which he found in the tomb. However, soon afterwards the High Duke died in an accident, and within weeks cases of vampirism were being reported throughout the region. Though the Duke's body was exhumed and destroyed, the phenomena continued and records claim that Arnold Paul turned a total of 17 other men and women into vampires.

Eighteenth Century
SERBIA (1725)

A vivid account of a plague of vampires which troubled several districts of Serbia for almost a decade has been described by John Heinrich Zopfius in a dissertation published in 1734: 'The Vampyres, which came out of the grave in the night-time, rushed upon people sleeping in their beds, sucked out all their blood, and destroyed them. They attacked men, women and children; sparing neither age nor sex. The people attacked by them complained of suffocation, and a great interception of spirits; after which, they soon expired. When these Vampyres were dug out of the graves, they appeared in all parts, such as the nostrils, cheeks, breasts, mouth, etc, turgid and full of blood. Their countenances were fresh and ruddy; and their nails, as well as their hair, very much grown. And, though they had been much longer dead than many other bodies, which were perfectly putrified, not the least mark of corruption was visible upon them. Those who were destroyed by them, after their death, became Vampyres; so that, to prevent so spreading an evil, it was found requisite to drive a stake through the dead body from whence, on this occasion, the blood flowed as if the person were alive. Sometimes the body was dug out of the grave, and burnt to ashes; upon which, all the disturbances ceased.'

MORAVIA (1731)

Two women, an old crone named Miliza and a young beauty, Stanno, both of whom had died in 1729, were believed to be the cause of an outbreak of vampirism at Metwett. Thirteen deaths occurred in a two-week period in this area, which were attributed to the couple. Miliza was said to have become a vampire as a result of having sexual intercourse with a male member of the Undead in Turkey before she moved to Moravia, and it was there that she infected her young confederate.

Nineteenth Century
YUGOSLAVIA (1816)

While the famous French author, Prosper Merimee, was dining with some friends at Varbeska, a vampire appeared at an upstairs window in the house and bit the neck of a young girl named Khava who was sleeping. According to

Merimee, the girl awoke just as the creature was raising himself up from her bed and, despite her fear, she recognised him as a man named Vieczany who had died a year before. At this, the family and some friends lit torches and went to the village cemetery where the man was buried. Vieczany's coffin was opened and his body was found to be untouched. Although the vampire was destroyed, his victim also passed away 18 days later.

AMERICA (1845)
According to a report in the *Norwich Courier* in Connecticut, after the death of a certain Horace Ray in Jewett City in the winter of 1845, the members of his family all fell ill of a wasting disease. When just one son remained alive, the body of the father was exhumed and found to be as fresh as the day it had been laid to rest. After the corpse had been burned, the health of the last member of the Ray family rapidly improved and he lived to a ripe old age convinced that his parent had been a vampire.

GREAT BRITAIN (1848)
A grisly-looking vampire plagued the Cranswell family living in isolated Croglin Grange in Cumberland. The creature repeatedly tried to break into the manor house and attack the beautiful young daughter, Anne. When finally tracked to its lair in a nearby churchyard by the girl's two brothers, the vampire's coffin was set on fire and its body consumed in the flames.

RUMANIA (1889)
One of the worst outbreaks of vampirism on record occurred in the district of Crassova when several dozen men, women and children were discovered to be slowly dying from loss of blood and bite marks on their necks. In a concerted effort by local people, a total of 30 corpses were interred in local graveyards and all pierced by stakes, before the attacks ceased. In Rumania, also, a few years later, the youngest-ever vampire was reported—a 13-year-old child who had recently died and was reportedly attacking other infants while they slept. The villagers of Prejam, in the Vilcea district, provided their own solution by staking the child in its coffin and then removing the head.

Twentieth Century
TRANSYLVANIA (1905)
When an old gypsy died in Capatineni, near Arges, where Vlad Dracula had once lived, it was noticed that no signs of rigor mortis developed while the body was on view to relatives and friends. When the corpse still remained supple after several days, it was decided the man had become a vampire and his heart was pierced by a stake before burial.

GREAT BRITAIN (1921)
A skeleton believed to be that of a woman, which was found in a garden in St Osyth in Essex, may have been that of a vampire—because the remains had

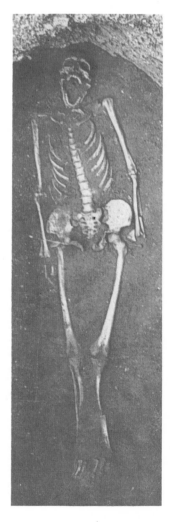

Skeleton of a suspected vampire found in Essex.

been bound with rope and nails driven through the thigh bones to prevent it from rising from the grave.

FRANCE (1926)

A vampire was reported to be on the loose at Nucourt near Gisors when a body completely drained of blood was discovered. The corpse was also covered in small teeth marks. This outrage matched reports of similar occurrences dating back at least a century, but despite extensive searches, no trace of the culprit has yet been found. In 1974, several tombs were discovered to have been rifled in this same locality.

YUGOSLAVIA (1936)

When several vampire attacks were reported in the vicinity of the castle of Herdody in Varazdin, an investigation led searchers to the grave of a young woman who had died in the thirteenth century. Although nothing was found in the tomb, when it was exorcised with holy water and prayers the attacks ceased.

GREAT BRITAIN (1970)

The famous London cemetery at Highgate was reported to be the haunt of a vampire after a series of strange events were reported, including the discovery of an unconscious young girl with small puncture marks on her neck. The events were said to emanate from a mysterious coffin from Turkey which had been buried in the cemetery the previous century—but despite a 'Vampire Hunt', the mystery has remained unsolved.

WEST GERMANY (1973)

A man described only as 'Mr Lorca' was confined to an institution for the criminally insane in Hamburg following a series of vampire attacks. He was said to have spent his days lying in a coffin, ate only raw meat, and at night attacked sleeping victims, biting them in the throat. It was also reported that he believed he was possessed by the spirit of Vlad Dracula.

AMERICA (1974)

The Weird Museum in Hollywood, California, claimed to have purchased the missing skeleton of Vlad Dracula, last seen in his tomb at the monastery in Snagov. The remains have been studied by two experts, Carl C. Francis, a professor of anatomy, and medical examiner George Gerber, who believe them to be the genuine remains of a Wallachian prince—although there are those who think the depression in the rib cage where a stake *might* once have been, and the long canine teeth of the skeleton, are just a little *too* good to be true!

III

I Like Playing Dracula

by Bela Lugosi
(1935)

I like playing 'horror' parts on the screen. This may surprise you, but let me explain my point of view.

There is a popular idea that portraying a monster of the Dracula type requires no acting ability. People are apt to think that anyone who likes to put on a grotesque make-up can be a fiend. That is wrong.

A monster, to be convincing, must have a character and a brain.

The screen monster produced by mere tricks of make-up and lighting will never thrill an audience. It will make them laugh! It is just a machine which does not understand what it is doing.

Now, imagine this creature with a character, with reasoning power and certain human mental facilities. It is no longer a machine. It can think.

Such a monster is able to thrill an audience. It can plot against the hero and heroine. It is a menace which must be combated by brains, not by running away.

We are all more afraid of cunning than brute force. Therefore, the monster must have cunning to trap his victims—physical strength is not enough to convince an audience.

Now, perhaps, you begin to see why I find the playing of fiends interesting!

When I am given a new rôle in a horror film, I have a character to create just as much as if I were playing a straight part.

Whether one thinks of films like *Dracula* as 'hokum' or not does not alter the fact; the horror actor *must* believe in his part. The player who portrays a film monster with his tongue in his cheek is doomed to failure.

An example of this occurred not very long ago. An actor, whose name I will not mention, played the part of a sinister foreign villain. He had been used to straight parts, and he went into this film laughing at himself. He did the correct villainous actions, but he had his tongue in his cheek all the time.

The villain was completely unconvincing and as a result the film was a flop at the box office. Later, an almost exactly similar character was played by another actor. He took it seriously. Audiences believed in the villain and the film was a success.

I am not saying that I personally take seriously these vampires and monsters as such. I am saying that one must take them seriously when one is portraying them.

In playing Dracula, I have to work myself up into believing that he is real, to ascribe to myself the motives and emotions that such a character would feel. For a time I *become* Dracula—not merely an actor playing at being a vampire.

A good actor will 'make' a horror part. He will build up the character until it convinces him and he is carried away by it.

There are, of course, plenty of tricks of the trade to be employed, such as effective make-up, clever photography, a threatening voice and claw-like gestures with the hands. These are important in the 'hokum' film and must be used. But even they must be employed with intelligence or they will fail to thrill.

To leave the theoretical discussion of so-called monsters, there is another reason why I do not mind being 'typed' in eerie thrillers.

With few exceptions, there are, among actors, only two types who matter at the box office. They are heroes and villains. The men who play these parts are the only ones whose names you will see in electric lights outside the theatre.

Obviously, I cannot play a juvenile part—you will not find me competing with Clark Gable or Robert Montgomery! Therefore, I have gone to the other extreme in my search for success and public acclaim.

Every year a number of films with fantastic or supernatural characters are made, and will, it seems, continue to be made, whatever may happen to the horror 'cycle' of pictures. I have deliberately specialised in such characters— and I firmly believe there will be suitable rôles for me for a long time to come!

Bela Lugosi as he looked when he visited England in 1951.

❧ IV ❧

The Dracula Films

*A Chronological Checklist of
the major movies based on
Bram Stoker's character*

Vampires have featured in literally hundreds of motion pictures, from the early days of silent films right up to the present day. The following list, however, concentrates on those films which were directly inspired by Stoker's work, even if, in some cases, the names of the leading characters were altered.

*   *   *

NOSFERATU: Eine Symphonie des Grauens (*Prana Films, Germany. 1922*)
Directed by F. W. Murnau. Screenplay by Henrik Galeen.
Starring: Max Schreck (Count Orlok), Gustav von Wagenheim, Greta Schröder-Matray, Alexander Granach, Georg H. Schnell, Ruth Landshoff.

DRACULA (*Universal Pictures, USA. 1931*)
Directed by Tod Browning. Screen play by Garrett Fort.
Starring: Bela Lugosi (Dracula), Edward Van Sloan, Helen Chandler, David Manners, Dwight Frye.

DRACULA (*Universal Pictures, USA. 1931. Spanish language version filmed simultaneously with the above*)
Directed by George Melford.
Starring: Carlos Villarias (Dracula), Lupita Tovar, Carmen Guerrero, Alvarez Rubia, Barry Norton.

MARK OF THE VAMPIRE (*MGM, USA. 1935*)
Directed by Tod Browning. Screenplay by Guy Endore and Bernard Schubert.
Starring: Bela Lugosi (Count Mora), Carol Borland, Lionel Barrymore, Elizabeth Allan, Lionel Atwill, Jean Hersholt.

DRACULA'S DAUGHTER (*Universal Pictures, USA. 1936*)
Directed by Lambert Hillyer. Screenplay by Garrett Fort and Oliver Jeffries based on Bram Stoker's short story 'Dracula's Guest'.

Starring: Gloria Holden (Countess Marya Zaleska), Edward Van Sloan, Otto Kruger, Marguerite Churchill, Irving Pichel, Hedda Hopper.

SON OF DRACULA (*Universal Pictures, USA. 1943*)
Directed by Robert Siodmak. Screenplay by Eric Taylor and Curt Siodmak.
Starring: Lon Chaney jnr. (Count Alucard—Dracula backwards!), Robert Paige, Louise Allbritton, Evelyn Ankers, Frank Craven.

RETURN OF THE VAMPIRE (*Columbia Pictures, USA. 1943*)
Directed by Lew Landers. Screenplay by Griffin Jay and Kurt Neumann.
Starring: Bela Lugosi (Armand Tesla), Nina Foch, Frieda Inescort, Miles Mander, Roland Varno.

HOUSE OF FRANKENSTEIN (*Universal Pictures, USA. 1944*)
Directed by Erle C. Kenton. Screenplay by Edward T. Lowe and Curt Siodmak.
Starring: John Carradine (Baron Latoes), Boris Karloff, Lon Chaney jnr., Anne Gwynne, J. Carroll Naish, Lionel Atwill, George Zucco, Glenn Strange.

HOUSE OF DRACULA (*Universal Pictures, USA. 1945*)
Directed by Erle C. Kenton. Screenplay by Edward T. Lowe.
Starring: John Carradine (Baron Latoes), Lon Chaney jnr., Martha O'Driscoll, Lionel Atwill, Glenn Strange.

ABBOTT AND COSTELLO MEET FRANKENSTEIN (*Universal Pictures, USA. 1948*)
Directed by Charles Barton. Screenplay by Robert Lees, Frederic Rinaldo and John Grant.
Starring: Bela Lugosi (Dracula), Bud Abbott, Lou Costello, Lenore Aubert, Lon Chaney jnr., Glenn Strange.

DRAKULA INSTANBULDA (*Demirag Studios, Turkey. 1953*)
Directed by Mehmet Muhtar. Screenplay by Unit Deniz, based on Bram Stoker's *Dracula* and *The Impaling Voivode* by Ali Riga Seifi. Combines the novel and the legend of Vlad the Impaler.
Starring: Alif Kaptan (Vlad/Dracula), Annie Ball, Turgut Demirag.

THE RETURN OF DRACULA (*United Artists, USA. 1958*)
Directed by Paul Landres. Screenplay by Pat Fiedler.
Starring: Francis Lederer (Bellac), Norma Eberhardt, Ray Stricklyn.

DRACULA (or THE HORROR OF DRACULA) (*Hammer Films, UK. 1958*)
Directed by Terence Fisher. Screenplay by Jimmy Sangster.
Starring: Christopher Lee (Dracula), Peter Cushing, Michael Gough, Melissa Stribling, Carol Marsh, John Van Eyssen.

BRIDES OF DRACULA (*Hammer Films, UK. 1960*)
Directed by Terence Fisher. Screenplay by Jimmy Sangster, Peter Bryan and Edward Percy.
Starring: David Peel (Baron Meinster), Peter Cushing, Martita Hunt, Yvonne Monlaur, Freda Jackson, Miles Malleson, Andrée Melly.

KISS OF THE VAMPIRE (*Hammer Films, UK. 1963*)
Directed by Don Sharp. Screenplay by John Elder (*pseud.* Anthony Hinds).
Starring: Noel Willman (Count Ravna), Clifford Evans, Jennifer Daniel, Isobel Black.

DRACULA—PRINCE OF DARKNESS (or BLOOD FOR DRACULA) (*Hammer Films, UK. 1965*)
Directed by Terence Fisher. Screenplay by John Samson.
Starring: Christopher Lee (Dracula), Barbara Shelley, Andrew Keir, Francis Matthews, Charles Tingwell, Thorley Walters.

BILLY THE KID VERSUS DRACULA (*Circle Productions/Embassy, USA. 1966*)
Directed by William Beaudine. Screenplay by Karl Hittleman.
Starring: John Carradine (Dracula), Chuck Courtney, Melinda Plowman.

A TASTE OF BLOOD (or THE SECRET OF DR ALUCARD) (Creative Films Inc., USA. 1967)
Directed by Herschell Gordon Lewis. Screenplay by Donald Standford.
Starring: Bill Rogers (Alucard/Dracula), Elizabeth Wilkinson, Otto Schlesinger, Ted Schell, Gail Janis.

DRACULA HAS RISEN FROM THE GRAVE (*Hammer Films, UK. 1968*)
Directed by Freddie Francis. Screenplay by John Elder.
Starring: Christopher Lee (Dracula), Veronica Carlson, Barry Andrews, Rupert Davies, Ewan Hopper, Barbara Ewing.

BLOOD OF DRACULA'S CASTLE (*A & E Film Corporation, USA. 1969*)
Directed by Al Adamson. Screenplay by Rex Carlton.
Starring: Alex D'Arcy (Count Townsend), John Carradine, Paula Raymond.

JONATHAN, VAMPIRE STERBEN NICHT (*Beta Films, Germany. 1970*)
Directed by Hans W. Geissendorfer. Screenplay by H. W. Geissendorfer.
Starring: Paul Albert Krumm (Dracula), Jurgen Jung, Greta Langen.

THE MASTER OF THE DUNGEON (*Merrick International, USA. 1970*)
Directed by Laurence Merrick. Screenplay by Wilson Carter.
Starring: Des Roberts (Dracula), Claudia Barron, John Landon, Frank Donato.

Christopher Lee in *Dracula Has Risen from the Grave* (1968).

THE HEIRESS OF DRACULA (or THE STRANGE ADVENTURE OF JONATHAN HARKER) (*Telecine, German/Spanish co-production. 1970*)
Directed by Jess Franco. Screenplay by Andrew Williams based on Bram Stoker's short story, 'Dracula's Guest'.
Starring: Susann Korda, Dennis Price, Paul Muller, Ewa Stroemberg, Soledad Miranda.

COUNT DRACULA (or EL CONDE DRACULA and BRAM STOKER'S COUNT DRACULA) (*American-International. 1970*)
Directed by Jess Franco. Screenplay by Harry Alan Towers.
Starring: Christopher Lee (Dracula), Herbert Lom, Fred Williams, Soledad Miranda, Klaus Kinski.

TASTE THE BLOOD OF DRACULA (*Hammer-Warner Pathé, UK. 1970*)
Directed by Peter Sasdy. Screenplay by John Elder.
Starring: Christopher Lee (Dracula), Ralph Bates, Geoffrey Keen, John Carson, Peter Sallis, Linda Hayden, Isla Blair, Martin Jarvis.

SCARS OF DRACULA (*Hammer Films, UK. 1970*)
Directed by Roy Ward Baker. Screenplay by John Elder.
Starring: Christopher Lee (Dracula), Christopher Matthews, Anoushka Hempel, Dennis Waterman, Jenny Hanley, Patrick Troughton.

LAKE OF DRACULA (or CHI O SUU MI) (*Toho, Japan. 1971*)
Directed by Michio Yamamoto. Screenplay by M. Yamamoto.
Starring: Shigen Amachi (Dracula), Yoko Mihara, Keinosuke Wada. (*The first Japanese version of Bram Stoker's novel.*)

DRACULA AD 1972 (*Hammer-Warner Pathé, UK. 1972*)
Directed by Alan Gibson. Screenplay by Don Houghton.
Starring: Christopher Lee (Dracula), Peter Cushing, Christopher Neame, Stephanie Beacham, Caroline Munro, Marsha Hunt.

BLACULA (*American-International, USA. 1972*)
Directed by William Crain. Screenplay by Joseph T. Naar and William Marshall.
Starring: Charles Macauley (Dracula), William Marshall (Prince Mamuwalde), Vonette McGee, Elisha Cook jnr., Denise Nichols. (*The first Black version of Dracula.*)

THE SATANIC RITES OF DRACULA (*Hammer-Warner Pathé, UK. 1973*)
Directed by Alan Gibson. Screenplay by John Elder.
Starring: Christopher Lee (Dracula), Peter Cushing, Joanna Lumley.

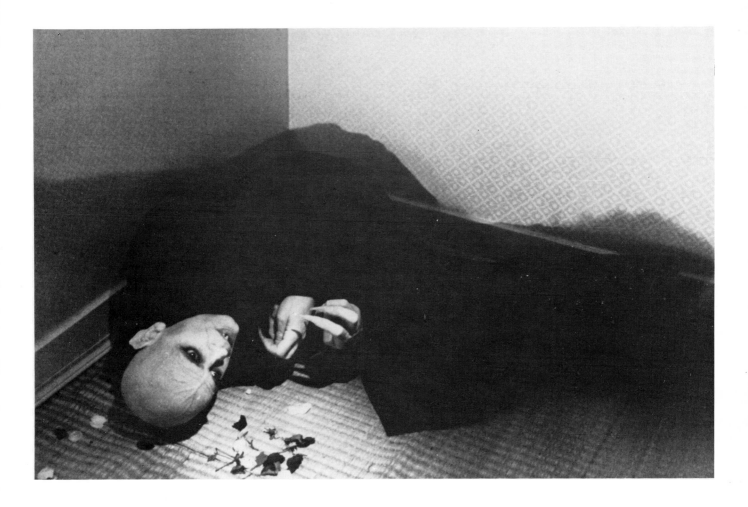

DRACULA (or BRAM STOKER'S DRACULA) (*Curtis Productions, USA. 1973*)
Directed by Dan Curtis. Screenplay by Richard Matheson.
Starring: Jack Palance (Dracula), Simon Ward, Nigel Davenport, Penelope Horner, Pamela Brown, Fiona Lewis, Murray Brown.

SCREAM, BLACULA, SCREAM (*American-International, USA. 1973*)
Directed by Bob Kelljan. Screenplay by Joseph T. Naar.
Starring: William Marshall (Blacula), Richard Lawson, Pam Grier, Bernie Hamilton, Don Mitchell.

DRACULA'S SAGA (or LA SAGA DE LOS DRACULAS) (*Profilmes, Spain. 1973*)
Directed by Leon Klimovsky. Screenplay by Antonio Jerez.
Starring: Narciso Ibanez Menta (Dracula), Jean Molino, Dennis Price.

COUNTESS DRACULA (*American-International, USA. 1975*)
Directed by Roger Corman. Screenplay by William Ophen.
Starring: Sara Bey (Countess Dracula), Mark Damon, Philip Harris.

Klaus Kinski, as Count Orlok, meets his end in the 1979 version of *Nosferatu*.

155

BLOOD FOR DRACULA (*Andy Warhol Productions, USA. 1975*)
Directed and written by Paul Morrisey.
Starring: Udo Kier (Dracula), Joe Dallesandro, Maxine McKendry, Vittorio De Sica, Arno Juerging.

DRACULA: FATHER AND SON (or DRACULA: PERE ET FILS) (*Molinaro Films, France. 1977*)
Directed and written by Edouard Molinaro.
Starring: Christopher Lee (Dracula), Bernard Menez, Catherine Breillet.

TENDER DRACULA (or TENDRE DRACULA) (*VM Productions, France. 1977*)
Directed by Pierre Grunstein. Screenplay by Alain Robbe-Grillet.
Starring: Peter Cushing (Dracula), Bernard Menez, Stephane Shandor, Julien Guiomar, Nathalie Courval, Alida Valli.

NOSFERATU—PHANTOM DER NACHT (*Twentieth Century Fox, USA. 1979*)
Directed and written by Werner Herzog.
Starring: Klaus Kinski (Nosferatu), Isabelle Adjani, Bruno Ganz.

DRACULA (*Universal Pictures, USA. 1979*)
Directed by John Badham. Screenplay by W. D. Richter.
Starring: Frank Langella (Dracula), Lord Olivier, Kate Nelligan, Donald Pleasence.

COUNTESS DOLINGEN OF GRATZ (or LES JEUX DE LA COMTESSE DOLINGEN DE GRATZ) (*Graphis Films, France. 1981*)
Directed and written by Catherine Binet based on 'Dracula's Guest' by Bram Stoker.
Starring: Catherine Mathilde (Countess Dolingen), Pierre Foss, Henri Chamion.

V

Vampires—The Mystery Diagnosed

by Dr David H. Dolphin

An explanation for the vampire's habits and bloodthirsty compulsions as immortalised in Bram Stoker's novel *Dracula* has been advanced by Dr David H. Dolphin, a Canadian biochemist working at the University of British Columbia. His extensive research into the controversial subject was made public in a paper he delivered before the American Association for the Advancement of Science in Los Angeles in May 1985.

Dr Dolphin's pronouncements generated widespread publicity and caused one Washington correspondent, Alex Brummer, to declare, 'The scoffers who chortled their way through hundreds of late-night vampire films may soon be hanging garlic around their necks and praying for daybreak. For new research suggests that the horrific folklore figure that has laced literature and culture since the Middle Ages may, in fact, have suffered from a rare genetic disease.'

In his paper, Dr Dolphin advanced the theory that vampires are actually men or women who suffer from one of a class of incurable hereditary diseases known as the porphyrias—of which there are at least eight. At the core of porphyria is a deficiency of haeme, the red blood pigment produced in the liver which helps to carry oxygen in haemoglobin.

As a result of this malfunction in the body chemicals, said Dr Dolphin, sufferers became afflicted with precisely the same symptoms that trouble the 'Children of the Night', as the vampires of literature are generally known. Their bodies became grotesquely disfigured and they evidenced extreme sensitivity to any form of light.

Even mild exposure to ordinary sunlight caused victims to run the risk of having their skin disfigured by sores and scars. Sometimes, the nose and fingers would actually fall off, and a victim's hands could come to resemble an animal's paws. Lips and gums would also become so stretched and tightened that the teeth—though no larger than those of ordinary people—would stick out, giving the appearance of fearful, animal-like fangs.

It was because of this, said Dr Dolphin, that victims of the disease would only venture out at night. They might also grow all their body hair long as a protection against the light. And—most controversially of all—he argued that porphyria victims in the past instinctively sought the haeme their bodies needed, but could not make themselves, by biting and sucking the blood of others.

157

The mystery of
vampirism solved—or
is it?

Today, with one in 200,000 people suffering from this disease, one form of treatment used is the injection of haeme. In the Middle Ages, however, less travel and more inbreeding might have led to porphyria becoming concentrated in certain areas—and with it the development of the vampire legend.

The biochemist also offered an explanation for the universal belief that once a victim had been bitten by a vampire he or she was similarly smitten with the blood-lust. The reason for this was that brothers and sisters of the vampire might have shared the same defective genes, and while the symptoms generally lay dormant, the shock of a bite from an open carrier of the disease may have released the vampire characteristics in the sibling.

Stressful events were very much the key to this occurring, said Dr Dolphin, and anyone who lost a lot of blood would certainly be under considerable stress. He supported this assertion by citing the now established fact that porphyria attacks can be triggered by alcohol or drugs.

The popular method used by people to defend themselves against the attacks of vampires by utilising garlic was also explainable by logic. For the plant contains dialkyl disulphide, which is very similar to the chemicals that are now known to severely aggravate the symptoms of porphyria by destroying a haeme protein called P450.

This would be reason enough for anyone suffering from vampirism to avoid the malodorous root, said Dr Dolphin. He would not, however, speculate on the efficiency of using silver bullets or crucifixes to achieve the same ends!

The biochemist admitted that he could not refute the evidence that haeme could not, apparently, pass through the stomach wall into the blood stream when drunk through the mouth—although he did claim that cattle's blood was drunk in modern Transylvania to combat porphyria symptoms.

The subject of vampires was one enshrined in myth and legend, Dr Dolphin concluded, and although he hoped his work had thrown up some new ideas, there was still much work to be done on the mystery of the terrible night creature and his 'kiss of undeath'.

✦ VI ✦

Dracula Societies

ENGLAND

The Dracula Society
Hon Sec: Robert James Leake, 36 Elliston House, 100 Wellington Street,
   Woolwich, London SE18 6QF.
The Count Dracula Fan Club
Founder: John Raven, BM Dracula, London WC1N 3XX.
The Dracula Experience
9 Marine Parade, Whitby YO21 3PR. *Run by:* Castlegate Exhibitions (York)
   Ltd., Lower Friargate, York YO1 1SL.

UNITED STATES OF AMERICA

The Count Dracula Society
President: Dr Donald A. Reed, 334 West 54th Street, Los Angeles, California
   90037.
The Gothick Gateway
Gordon R. Guy, 22 Canterbury Street, East Hartford, Connecticut 06118.
Vampire Information Exchange
Secretary: Dorothy Nixon, Box 6459, Rochester, NY 14627.